A
New Testament Walk
with Oswald Chambers

A
NEW TESTAMENT WALK
WITH OSWALD CHAMBERS

Oswald Chambers

Compiled by James R. Adair
and Harry Verploegh

Fleming H. Revell
A Division of Baker Book House
Grand Rapids, Michigan 49516

© 1992, 1994 by James R. Adair and Harry Verploegh

Published by Fleming H. Revell
a division of Baker Book House Company
P.O. Box 6287, Grand Rapids, MI 49516-6287
All rights reserved

One-volume revision of *101 Days in the Gospels with Oswald Chambers* and
101 Days in the Epistles with Oswald Chambers

Second printing, October 1998

Printed in the United States of America

Library of Congress Cataloging-in-Publication Data
Chambers, Oswald, 1874–1917.
    A New Testament walk with Oswald Chambers / Oswald Chambers ;
compiled by James R. Adair and Harry Verploegh.
        p.   cm.
    ISBN 0-8007-1753-8
    1. Bible. N.T.—Meditations. 2. Bible. N.T.—Quotations. 3. Bible.
N.T.—Devotional literature. I. Adair, James R., 1923– . II. Verploegh, Harry. III. Title.
BS2341.3.C48 1998
242'.5—dc21   97-37467

For current information about all releases from Baker Book House, visit
our web site:

http://www.bakerbooks.com

∼ CONTENTS ∼

∼ FOREWORD ∼

I first "met" Oswald Chambers when I was in prep school. The campus librarian, a grandmotherly type, knew my love for books, and for a birthday gift she gave me a copy of the daily devotional *My Utmost for His Highest,* Chambers's most renowned work.

The man, of course, had been dead for forty years at that point, so you must understand that our introduction was a matter of my engaging him through his writings. When my friend the librarian brought us together, I had no clue that Chambers would become someone who would nourish me through the best and worst days of my life. So attached to him would I become that I would later refer to him as simply OC when I reflected on his words in my journal.

I must be candid to say that I was disappointed in the first encounters I had with OC because his words, which often challenged one to wait upon God in silence, were so adverse to my activist, make-it-all-happen-yourself mind-set. I neglected him for many months at a time and got back in touch only when I felt a surge of spiritual hunger or curiosity.

A second copy of Chambers's best-selling book came to me years later as a wedding gift. For the first months of our married life, Gail and I frequently looked into *My Utmost,* and I discovered that my friend was making more and more sense to me. OC tends to make that happen in the life of one who is getting older and feeling more and more beat up by the realities of life.

Since then I have received many more copies of Chambers's *Utmost* as gifts. And I have enjoyed using each one—marking the pages, underlining phrases, and writing blunt little notes to myself such as "He's sure got your number on this one."

Then there came the day when I spent several hours in delightful conversation with an aged woman, Dorothy Docking, who had known Oswald Chambers when she was a small girl. "Tell me everything you remember," I said. And she did.

From her I learned that OC was a highly artistic man who could become consumed with the beauties of creation. Indeed, a reading of his journals (which I pursued much later) reveals this side of him when he goes to great lengths to describe the shadows and colors of a sunset on the Egyptian desert.

I learned that Chambers was a man with a brilliant mind and wit and that he could seize and mold the minds and spirits of tough men when he gave lectures on the Bible and on the classics. I learned that Chambers was a mentor to young people, a lover of children, and a shepherd to soldiers. Having heard all that, I returned to his writings and began to read everything that had been put into print under his name.

But this friendship with Oswald Chambers did not reach its peak until I went through a deep personal trough in my life and was in great need of God's mercy. My sense of loss and shame was indescribable. Turning to my old friend, I began to realize that he must have known some deep personal losses of his own. No man could have written with the sensitivity and understanding of the restorative grace and kindness of Christ as he did unless he had one day drawn upon his own losses. That was a part of Chambers I had not seen until I was in great need.

At that time I heard Chambers say (and I am paraphrasing), "When God permits you to be stripped of everything to do with your exterior life and work, He desires that you enhance the activities of your interior." I heard my friend encouraging me to seek silence, an enhanced intercessory life, and a deeper sense of the majesty of God. In just a sentence or two, OC had revitalized me with a sense of purpose and mission that no one could deny. There would be others swift to judge, quick to provide answers, and sharp to think that they understood causes and consequences. But Chambers understood that a person's worst moments can be (in some cases) God's greatest opportunity to develop a person after His own heart. Themes of God's redeeming love began to leap out at me from all of Chambers's books, and I came to consider this man— even though he died more than twenty years before I was born—as among my closest friends.

I am delighted, therefore, to commend to you my "friend" Oswald Chambers and this book containing many of his insightful comments. He speaks to you and me out of his years among students and fighting men. He speaks from his days on the North African desert, which he loved, where he clearly derived many of his metaphors and appreciations of God's grandeur. He speaks from pain, from silence, from disciplined thought, and from a highly intimate journey with Jesus. In your desert moments and in your spiritually curious hours, drink deeply from his well.

Gordon MacDonald

❧ PREFACE ❧

In this book, you have ahead of you a delightful spiritual journey of 202 days in the Gospels and Epistles with Oswald Chambers, the beloved minister of the late 1800s and early 1900s. He is especially known for his classic devotional *My Utmost for His Highest*. You will read designated passages from your Bible and then reflect on comments by Chambers that cast light on one key thought in each Scripture portion. Normally, you should be able to complete each daily reading in less than ten minutes, though you will likely want to take more time to contemplate the incisive comments relating to the selected verse from the Scripture you have read.

Most of Chambers's statements come from a vast collection that my longtime friend Harry Verploegh (ver-plew) has excerpted from the author's thirty-four books. A few excerpts are from articles Chambers wrote for *God's Revivalist and Bible Advocate*, published by God's Bible School, Cincinnati, where he taught for a time in the early 1900s.

Harry became intensely interested in the writings of Chambers after he retired from the business world in the late 1970s and began avidly reading works of the "saints and sages of the ages." Both of us had been

11

acquainted with Chambers before then, but Harry's reading extended from *My Utmost for His Highest* to Chambers's other thirty-three books. As Harry got deeper into Chambers, he would tell me, "Nobody says it quite like Chambers!" He began marking and clipping excerpts and mounting them on subject cards and, eventually, had more than ten thousand Chambers quotations. In addition, he clipped from the writings of many others, until at last count he had well over one hundred thousand quotations mounted on cards. At age eighty-nine, he continues to read, clip, and paste.

At times as I visited him in the retirement home where he resides, Harry enthusiastically shared some of the quotations he clipped from Chambers's books. The result: We eventually compiled two books containing many of the excerpts, *101 Days in the Gospels with Oswald Chambers* and *101 Days in the Epistles with Oswald Chambers*. Both are now out of print. In this volume, you will find key verses and selected quotations from the previously mentioned books.

The first 101 Scripture readings from the Gospels follow a chronology contained in Kermit Zarley's *The Gospels Interwoven* published by Victor Books in 1987. His chronology is based on the majority view of thirteen leading parallel-column harmonies of the four Gospels appearing in English over the past 325 years. The next 101 readings take you through the Epistles of Paul, James, Peter, and John.

The quotations from Chambers's writings have been edited to reflect modern punctuation and spelling. Pronouns referring to deity are capitalized. Bible quotations in excerpts are from a version of the King James Bible in use in the early 1900s.

Harry and I hope and pray that God will use this book to deepen your walk with Him, and that you will enjoy it enough to share the book with others. Many people, including some couples, have told us that they have delighted in using the former *101* books in daily devotionals.

James R. Adair

~ INTRODUCTION ~

OSWALD CHAMBERS: HIGH CLIMBER

Even as a child, Oswald Chambers had utmost confidence in God. After he had gone to bed, older members of his family enjoyed listening to him pray as they stood on the stairway near his room. Once he asked God to send him two wild guinea pigs for pets, and morning after morning he inspected the chicken run to see if his visitors had arrived. Certain that God would not disappoint him, he continued to watch until finally, to his great delight, one morning he discovered two of the furry little animals. His childlike faith and simplicity remained the same throughout life.

Oswald Chambers was born July 24, 1874, in Aberdeen, Scotland, the fourth son of Clarence and Hannah Chambers. His father pastored a Baptist church in Aberdeen and later served churches in Stoke-on-Trent and Perth; his last pastorate was in London.

Chambers unashamedly gave tribute to his parents for his godly heritage. When he was a student at the University of Edinburgh, he wrote, "God is the mover, prime and sole, above and through circumstances. I feel traits in my character I knew not of before, and it causes me to bow in deeper gratitude for that home training.

. . . Indeed we do not know how deep a debt we owe to our mothers and fathers and their training."

After he entered his teens and was living in London, Chambers heard Charles Haddon Spurgeon preach. On the way home, he mentioned to his father that had there been an opportunity at the close of the service, he would have given himself to the Lord. His father responded, "You can do it now, my boy," and there in the street beneath a gas lamp, Oswald opened his heart to Christ. Oswald was baptized and joined a Baptist church where his family attended. In time he became a Sunday school teacher and during the week ministered the gospel to men—some of them ex-convicts—in lodging homes and missions.

In his early years, Chambers blossomed as a musician and an artist. In Perth, he began his schooling in Sharp's Institute, and here drawing became a marked joy. While in Infants' Class, he drew a large golden eagle in chalks that remained on exhibit for several days.

When he was eighteen, Chambers earned an Art Master's Certificate, enabling him to teach and illustrate for his livelihood. He won a scholarship for study abroad but turned it down, noting that such ventures wrecked some men both morally and physically. Instead, he studied fine art and architecture at the University of Edinburgh. At the age of twenty-two, however, he decided to study for the ministry, following the counsel of several Scottish men of God. On November 11, 1896, he penned: "It would be playing with the sacred touch of God to neglect or stifle this strange yet deep conviction that sometime I must be a minister."

Chambers entered the Scottish Dunoon Training College in 1897 and took a dominating position. Within a year, he became a tutor in logic, moral philosophy, and psychology. In 1900, he prepared and published a booklet titled *Outlines for the Study of Historical Philosophy*. He also started a Browning Society, encouraging students and townspeople to become enthusiastic readers of the poetry of Robert Browning.

He became president of Christian Endeavor, leading special prayer meetings for young people and conducting a young men's enquiry meeting on Sundays at the college, where he would sit with students and talk as one friend to another. One student recalled that "the table-talk [with Chambers] taught us how to cultivate the art of conversation. Ability to change the theme and lift the conversation to a more elevated plane was characteristic of Mr. Chambers. Without monopolizing the conversation, he would regulate it and charm and entertain us all."

In 1902, Chambers began to concentrate more and more on being totally God's man, sharing with others the message of redemption in Christ that, along with sanctification, became so much the theme of his preaching and writings. He began to minimize such side interests as art, poetry, music, and philosophy, giving himself to more preaching. For a time his messages struck terror in the hearts of his hearers instead of confidence and love. However, in time, as he supplied pulpits in various parts of Scotland, his intensity and vehemence gradually mellowed.

By this time Chambers was a tall, slender young man with a gaunt face and piercing gray-blue eyes set under a broad cleft of brow; his mouth was firm, his lips thin, and his accent decidedly Scottish. A friend at Dunoon College wrote that "the whole together might have given an impression of austerity, but on the contrary; the countenance was unusually pleasing and inviting. This decided cast of features gave him a look older than his years," though at times "he looked a mere youth" and another time "a man of maturer years."

Without doubt, Chambers passed through definite phases in his spiritual climb. He often said, "Consistency is the hobgoblin of little minds." During a period at Dunoon, he often tramped the Scottish hills with feelings of being a wretch far from God. Though God obviously used him to reach others for Christ, Chambers described that period as "four years of hell on earth." A friend observed: "In his own soul there was darkness and misery" and "he had never believed possible what the sinful disposition in him was capable of."

Yet Chambers was persuaded that there was more to Christianity than he had experienced, prompting him to write:

> Let me climb, let me climb, I'm sure I've time,
> 'Ere the mist comes up from the sea;
> Let me climb in time to the height sublime;
> Let me reach where I long to be.

Then came the day when Chambers abandoned himself absolutely to God, advancing to a new plateau of spiritual fullness that set him aflame in his remaining years to be an instrument of blessing to millions. While in Dunoon College as a tutor in philosophy, he heard Dr. F. B. Meyer speak about the Holy Spirit. Later in his room he asked God for the baptism of the Holy Spirit, "whatever that meant," he later wrote. Then followed the four years when God seemed distant and the Bible became "the dullest, most uninteresting book in existence," and Chambers saw the "vileness and bad-motivedness" of his nature.

During these valley years, he testified that God spoke to him only three times—and in unusual ways! First, as Chambers sat in his room one night, his collie came in through the window, put his head on his knee, looked into his master's eyes for a few minutes, then went out again. Another time, the youngest child of the family with whom Chambers lived, came to Oswald's room, barefoot and in his nightclothes, and said, "Mr. Chambers, I loves you," and went off to bed. Again, while Chambers was conducting a Christian Endeavor meeting, a mentally impaired girl laid a bunch of withered flowers on the table for him, with a piece of paper on which was written, "With love from Meg."

Finally, God spoke to him through Luke 11:13: "If ye then, being evil, know how to give good gifts to your children, how much more shall your Heavenly Father give the Holy Spirit to them that ask Him?" Though he had been born of the Spirit as a teenager, for a time Chambers viewed himself too unworthy to take God at His word to receive the fullness of the

Spirit. Days passed until at a mission meeting he "claimed the gift of the Holy Spirit in dogged committal on Luke 11:13." But he still felt "dry and empty as ever, no power or realization of God, no witness of the Holy Spirit," he declared.

Then as he talked with a friend, he realized that he "had been wanting power" in his own hand, so that he could say, "Look what I have by putting my all on the altar." And then and there his heart was "filled to overflowing with the love of God," he wrote.

"On various occasions Chambers warned against the imitation of the experience of some great soul," according to D. W. Lambert in his book *Oswald Chambers: An Unbribed Soul.* "What Paul, Augustine, Luther, and others went through were classic examples of how God could deal with souls in their desperate need, but they are not to be slavishly imitated. So we believe Chambers would not want any seeking soul to go through the long agony that was his until he came out into the glorious sunshine of the redeeming Christ. On the other hand his experience is a challenge to all for whom conversion and even sanctification have been but glib and superficial expressions."

From that time on, Oswald Chambers became a mighty messenger of God, not only in the British Isles but to thousands abroad. From 1906 to 1910, he made four trips to the United States, preaching at holiness camp meetings on the East coast and teaching for six months at God's Bible School in Cincinnati. This resulted in 181 articles, transcripts of his sermons and lectures, appearing in *God's Revivalist and Bible*

Advocate magazine between 1907 and 1916. Oswald and his wife, Gertrude (Biddy), spent a four-month honeymoon in the States following their marriage in May 1910. In later years, Biddy used her shorthand skills to record her husband's sermons, then began to publish them after his death.

After returning from their honeymoon, Chambers helped establish the Bible Training College in London, to prepare young people for the gospel ministry. However, in July 1915, the college was closed for the duration of World War I, and in October, Chambers sailed for Egypt to join the staff of the YMCA to minister to the Mediterranean Expeditionary Force at Zeitoun, seven miles outside Cairo. He was later joined there by Biddy and their daughter, Kathleen.

Here, for some two years he extended himself to the limits of his endurance as he ministered faithfully to British, Australian, and New Zealand forces stationed in Egypt during the Great War. Then in the fall of 1917 he fell suddenly ill and was rushed to a hospital in Cairo. An operation for appendicitis brought partial recovery. But on November 15, 1917, at the age of forty-three, Oswald Chambers heard God's call to the heavenly realms. A prophetic statement he had once written had come true: "I feel I shall . . . suddenly . . . flame out, do my work, and be gone."

A simple headstone in the military cemetery in Cairo marks his earthly resting place. On it: "A believer in Jesus Christ." Engraved on an open marble Bible at the base of the grave marker is his testimony taken from Luke 11:13: "How much more will your Heavenly Father give the Holy Spirit to them that ask Him?"

James R. Adair

Based on *Oswald Chambers: His Life and Work,* compiled by Biddy Chambers, 1933, 1938, 1959

∽ Key to Sources ∽

The sources of Oswald Chambers's quotations are indicated in each instance by the abbreviation of the title of the book from which the excerpt was taken. Page numbers shown relate to editions of Chambers's books published by Marshall, Morgan & Scott, London, England, and/or Christian Literature Crusade, Fort Washington, Pennsylvania.

In the source list, the word *Discovery* following titles and dates indicates Chambers's titles more recently published by Discovery House Publishers, Grand Rapids. *Zondervan* indicates titles published by Zondervan Publishing House, Grand Rapids. *Chosen* indicates books published by Chosen Books, Grand Rapids. In all cases, rights have been granted by the Oswald Chambers Publications Association.

AUG — *Approved unto God,* 1946, 1948, 1997, Discovery (combined with *Facing Reality*)

BFB — *Baffled to Fight Better,* 1931, 1990, Discovery

BE — *Biblical Ethics,* 1947

BP — *Biblical Psychology,* 1962, 1995, Discovery

BSG — *Bringing Sons unto Glory,* 1943, 1990, Discovery (combined with *Making All Things New*)

CD VOL. 1 — *Christian Discipline,* vol. 1, 1935, 1936, 1985, Zondervan

CD VOL. 2   *Christian Discipline,* vol. 2, 1935, 1936, 1986, Zondervan, one-volume edition, 1995, Discovery

CHI   *Conformed to His Image,* 1950, 1985, Chosen (1996, Discovery, combined with *The Servant as His Lord*)

DDL   *Devotions for a Deeper Life,* edited by Glenn D. Black (Grand Rapids: Francis Asbury Press, © 1986, God's Bible School)

DI   *Disciples Indeed,* 1955

GR   *God's Revivalist and Bible Advocate*

GW   *God's Workmanship,* 1953, 1997, Discovery

HGM   *He Shall Glorify Me,* 1946, 1997, Discovery

HG   *The Highest Good,* 1937, 1938, 1940, 1992, Discovery (combined with *The Shadow of an Agony*)

HRL   *His Resurrection and Our Life,* 1930, by Oswald Chambers Publications Association, combined with *Bringing Sons unto Glory, Making All Things New* © 1990, Discovery

IWP   *If Thou Wilt Be Perfect,* 1941

IYA   *If Ye Shall Ask,* 1958, 1985, Chosen (*If You Will Ask,* revised title, 1989, Discovery)

LG   *The Love of God,* 1938, 1973, 1985, Chosen (1988, Discovery)

MFL   *Moral Foundations of Life,* 1966

MUH   *My Utmost for His Highest,* © 1935, Dodd, Mead & Co.; © renewed by Oswald Chambers Publications Association, 1963 (1989, Discovery)

MUH-UE   *My Utmost for His Highest* (updated edition), © 1992 by Oswald Chambers Publications Association (Discovery)

NKW   *Not Knowing Whither,* 1934, 1989, Discovery (combined with *Our Portrait in Genesis* under the title *Not Knowing Where*)

OBH   *Our Brilliant Heritage,* 1929, 1930, 1931, 1975

OPG   *Our Portrait in Genesis,* 1957, 1989, Discovery (combined with *Not Knowing Where*)

PS   *The Philosophy of Sin,* 1960

PH   *The Place of Help,* © 1936, Dodd, Mead & Co., Grosset & Dunlap; 1989, Discovery

PR   *The Psychology of Redemption,* 1930, 1990, Discovery (under the title *Making All Things New,* combined with *Bringing Sons unto Glory*)

RTR   *Run Today's Race,* 1968 (previously *Seed Thoughts*)

SHL   *The Servant as His Lord,* 1957, 1996, Discovery (combined with *Conformed to His Image*)

SHH   *The Shade of His Hand,* 1936, 1991, Discovery

SA   *The Shadow of an Agony,* 1934, 1992, Discovery (combined with *The Highest Good*)

SSY   *So Send I You,* 1930, 1993, Discovery (combined with *Workmen of God*)

SH   *Still Higher for His Highest,* Zondervan by special arrangement with Marshall, Morgan & Scott, © 1970 D. W. Lambert

SSM   *Studies in the Sermon on the Mount,* 1960 (1996, Discovery)

WG   *Workmen of God,* 1937, 1993, Discovery (combined with *So Send I You*)

~ PART 1 ~
THE GOSPELS

CHRIST'S MINISTRY BEGINS

❧ I ❧

THE BEGINNING

READING: JOHN 1:1–18

The Word became flesh and made his dwelling among us.

JOHN 1:14

Jesus Christ is God-Man. God in essence cannot come anywhere near us. Almighty God does not matter to me; He is in the clouds. To be of any use to me, He must come down to the domain in which I live; and I do not live in the clouds but on the earth. The doctrine of the incarnation is that God did come down into our domain. The wisdom of God, the Word of God, the exact expression of God, was manifest in the flesh. That is the great doctrine of the New Testament—dust and deity made one. The pure gold of deity is of no use to us unless it is amalgamated in the right alloy—the pure divine working on the basis of the pure human: God and humanity one, as in our Lord Jesus Christ. There is only one God to the Christian, and His name is Jesus Christ, and in Him we see mirrored what the human race will be like on the basis of redemption—a perfect oneness between God and man. Jesus Christ has the power of reproducing Himself by regeneration, the power of introducing into us His own heredity, so that dust and deity again become one. SHH 9

29

∼ 2 ∼

BIRTHS OF JOHN THE BAPTIST
AND JESUS FORETOLD

READING: LUKE 1:1–56

The angel answered, "The Holy Spirit will come upon you, and the power of the Most High will overshadow you. So the holy one to be born will be called the Son of God."

LUKE 1:35

The tremendous revelation of Christianity is not the fatherhood of God, but the babyhood of God—God became the weakest thing in His own creation, and in flesh and blood He levered it back to where it was intended to be. No one helped Him; it was done absolutely by God manifest in human flesh. God has undertaken not only to repair the damage, but in Jesus Christ the human race is put in a better condition than when it was originally designed. It is necessary to understand these things if you are to be able to battle for your faith. SA 27

Adam is called the son of God. There is only one other "Son of God" in the Bible, and He is Jesus Christ. Yet we are called "sons of God," but how? In being reinstated through the atonement of Jesus Christ. BP 6

∼ 3 ∼

THE BIRTH OF JOHN THE BAPTIST
AND JOSEPH'S DREAM

READING: MATTHEW 1:18–25; LUKE 1:57–80

"She will give birth to a son, and you are to give him the name Jesus, because he will save his people from their sins."

MATTHEW 1:21

Jesus Christ is God manifest in the flesh, not a being with two personalities. He is the Son of God (the exact expression of Almighty God) and the Son of Man (the presentation of God's normal man). As the Son of God, He reveals what God is like; as the Son of Man, He mirrors what the human race will be like on the basis of redemption—a perfect oneness between God and man. SA 35

Jesus Christ was born *into* this world, not *from* it. He came into history from the outside of history; He did not evolve out of history. Our Lord's birth was an advent. He did not come from the human race; He came into it from above. Jesus Christ is not the best human being. He is a being who cannot be accounted for by the human race at all. He is God Incarnate, not man becoming God, but God coming into human flesh, coming into it from the outside. His life is the highest and the holiest entering in at the lowliest door. Our Lord entered history by the Virgin Mary. PR 29

～4～

THE BIRTH OF JESUS CHRIST

READING: LUKE 2:1–39

"Glory to God in the highest, and on earth peace to men on whom his favor rests."

LUKE 2:14

Jesus is the "Prince of Peace" because only in Him can men have God's goodwill and peace on earth. Thank God, through that beloved Son the great peace of God may come to every heart and to every nation under heaven, but it can come in no other way. None of us can ever have goodwill toward God if we won't listen to His Son. HGM 9

The coming of Jesus Christ is not a peaceful thing, it is a disturbing thing, because it means the destruction of every peace that is not based on a personal relationship to Himself. PH 61

~ 5 ~

JESUS' EARLY YEARS

READING: MATTHEW 2:1–23; LUKE 2:39–52
And the child grew and became strong; he was filled with wisdom, and the grace of God was upon him.
LUKE 2:40

The presentation of true Christian experience brings us face to face with spiritual beauty, a beauty which can never be forced or imitated, because it is a manifestation from within of a simple relationship to God that is being worked out all the time. There is nothing simple saving a man's relation to God in Christ, and that relationship must never be allowed to be complicated. Our Lord's childhood expresses this spiritual beauty: "And the Child grew, and waxed strong, becoming full of wisdom" (Luke 2:40). Jesus Christ developed in the way that God intended human beings to develop, and He exhibited the kind of life we ought to live when we have been born from above. SH 77

Jesus Christ came to make the great laws of God incarnate in human life; that is the miracle of God's grace. We are to be written epistles, "known and read of all men" (2 Cor. 3:2). There is no allowance whatever in the New Testament for the man who says he is saved by grace but who does not produce the graceful goods. Jesus Christ by His redemption can make our actual life in keeping with our religious profession. SSM 90

∼6∼

JOHN THE BAPTIST PREPARES THE WAY

READING: MATTHEW 3:1–17
(SUPPLEMENTARY READING: MARK 1:1–11; LUKE 3:1–23)
Then Jesus came from Galilee to the Jordan to be baptized by John.

MATTHEW 3:13

The baptism of our Lord was an extraordinary spiritual experience to Himself. "And there came a voice from heaven, saying, 'Thou art My beloved Son, in whom I am well pleased'" (Luke 3:22). We have no experience like that; it stands unique. There is only one beloved Son of God; we are sons of God through His redemption. PR 52

Jesus Christ is the true Baptizer; He baptizes with the Holy Ghost. He is the Lamb of God which taketh away the sin of the world—*my* sin. He is the One who can make me like Himself; the baptism of John could not do that. PR 49

At His baptism the Son of God as the Son of Man— as the whole human race rightly related to God—took on Himself the sin of the whole world; that is why He was baptized with John's baptism, which was a baptism of repentance from sin. PR 85

∽7∽

THE TEMPTATION OF JESUS

READING: MATTHEW 4:1–11
(SUPPLEMENTARY READING: MARK 1:12–13; LUKE 4:1–13)

Then Jesus was led by the Spirit into the desert to be tempted by the devil.

MATTHEW 4:1

We have to get rid of the idea that because Jesus was God He could not be tempted. Almighty God cannot be tempted, but in Jesus Christ we deal with God as man, a unique being—God-Man. It was as the Son of Man that "He fought the battle, and proved the possibility of victory." After His baptism, Satan, by the direct permission of the Holy Ghost, tested the faith of Jesus. "And straightway the Spirit driveth Him forth into the wilderness" (Mark 1:12). Satan broke what Adam held straight off, but he could not break what Jesus held in His person, though he tested Him in every conceivable way; therefore, having Himself "suffered being tempted, He is able to succor them that are tempted" (Heb. 2:18). CHI 56

Having "suffered being tempted," He knows how terrific are the onslaughts of the devil against human nature unaided; He has been there. Therefore, He can be touched with the feeling of our infirmities. God

Almighty was never "tempted in all points like as we are"—Jesus Christ was. CHI 99

∼8∼

THE LAMB OF GOD

READING: JOHN 1:19–34

The next day John saw Jesus coming toward him and said, "Look, the Lamb of God, who takes away the sin of the world!"

JOHN 1:29

In the days of His flesh, Jesus Christ exhibited this divine paradox of the Lion and the Lamb. He was the Lion in majesty, rebuking the winds and demons; He was the Lamb in meekness, "who when He was reviled, reviled not again" (1 Peter 2:23). He was the Lion in power, raising the dead; He was the Lamb in patience, who was "brought as a lamb to the slaughter, and as a sheep before her shearers is dumb, so He openeth not His mouth" (Isa. 53:7). He was the Lion in authority: "Ye have heard that it hath been said . . . but I say unto you"; He was the Lamb in gentleness: "Suffer the little children to come unto Me . . . and He took them up in His arms, put His hands upon them, and blessed them" (Mark 10:14, 16).

In our personal lives, Jesus Christ proves Himself to be all this: He is the Lamb to expiate our sins, to lift us out of condemnation and plant within us His own heredity of holiness; He is the Lion to rule over us, so that we gladly say, "The government of this life shall be upon His shoulders" (Isa. 9:6). And what is true in individual life is to be true also in the universe at large. The time is coming when the Lion of the tribe of Judah shall reign and when "the kingdoms of this world are become the kingdoms of our Lord, and of His Christ" (Rev. 11:15). CHI 121

∼9∼

JESUS REVEALS HIS GLORY AND AUTHORITY

READING: JOHN 2:1–25

So he made a whip . . . and drove all from the temple. . . . "Get these out of here! How dare you turn my Father's house into a market!"

JOHN 2:15–16

When the Lord visits the body of a man, the traffic in the man's soul awakens self-love, self-sympathy, and self-pity; and our Lord, who is the truth, scourges them out of the temple. (He does not scourge the temple.) He scourges the whole defiling crew that have no business there, out of the temple, and He says, "Make not My Father's house a house of merchandise." Note that phrase, "My Father's house." Talk about the dignity of the human body! Would that every one of us could realize, when we think of our own bodies, that Jesus Christ means that our bodies are His Father's house. And what did He accuse them of? He accused them of making "My Father's house a house of merchandise." Let this searching go home in every one of us. What am I doing in my body? Am I using my eyes, my ears, my tongue, my heart, my mind, my imagination for the glory and worship of God, or am I making merchandise for myself? The temple of God must be just and holy. When once the Lord has cleansed the defilement out of a man, there is no phrase that expresses his cleanness so marvelously as the phrase of the psalmist: "whiter than snow." GR 6/10/1910

∼ 10 ∼

JESUS TEACHES NICODEMUS

READING: JOHN 3:1–21
In reply Jesus declared, "I tell you the truth, no one can see the kingdom of God unless he is born again."
JOHN 3:3

Human earnestness and vowing cannot make a man a disciple of Jesus Christ any more than it can turn him into an angel; a man must receive something, and that is the meaning of being born again. When once a man is struck by his need of the Holy Spirit, God will put the Holy Spirit into his spirit. In regeneration, a man's personal spirit is energized by the Holy Spirit, and the Son of God is formed in him (Gal. 1:15–16; 4:19). This is the New Testament evangel, and it needs to be restated. New birth refers not only to a man's eternal salvation, but to his being of value to God in this order of things; it means infinitely more than being delivered from sin and from hell. The gift of the essential nature of God is made efficacious in us by the entering in of the Holy Spirit; He imparts to us the quickening life of the Son of God, and we are lifted into the domain where Jesus lives. LG 113

When we are born from above, the realization dawns that we are built for God, not for ourselves: "He hath made me." We are brought, by means of new birth, into the individual realization of God's great purpose for the human race, and all our small, miserable, parochial notions disappear. SSY 103

~ II ~

JOHN THE BAPTIST'S TESTIMONY ABOUT JESUS

READING: JOHN 3:22–36
He must become greater; I must become less.
JOHN 3:30

If you become a necessity to a soul, you are out of God's order. As a worker, your great responsibility is to be a friend of the Bridegroom. When once you see a soul in sight of the claims of Jesus Christ, you know that your influence has been in the right direction, and instead of putting out a hand to prevent the throes, pray that they grow ten times stronger until there is no power on earth or in hell that can hold that soul away from Jesus Christ. Over and over again, we become amateur providences; we come in and prevent God, and say, "This and that must not be." Instead of proving friends of the Bridegroom, we put our sympathy in the way, and the soul will one day say, "That one was a thief; he stole my affections from Jesus, and I lost my vision of Him."

Beware of rejoicing with a soul in the wrong thing, but see that you do rejoice in the right thing. "The friend of the Bridegroom . . . rejoiceth greatly because of the Bridegroom's voice: this my joy therefore is fulfilled. He must increase, but I must decrease" (John 3:29–30). MUH 84

∽ 12 ∽

JESUS TALKS WITH A SAMARITAN WOMAN

READING: JOHN 4:1–42

"Whoever drinks the water I give him will never thirst.
Indeed, the water I give him will become in him a spring
of water welling up to eternal life."

JOHN 4:14

Are you in constant contact with frozen natures in
your own family, in your business, in your friendships?
You have talked with them, prayed with them; you have
done everything you know how, but there is not the
slightest sign of conviction of sin, no trouble of conscience or heart. They are not "out-and-out" sinners,
but you know that they are "in-and-in" sinners; you
know they are wrong and twisted and have things that
are not clean, but you cannot make them realize it; they
always get away, frozen and untouched. Then bring your
own soul face to face with Jesus Christ: "Lord do *I*
believe that Thou canst thaw that man's nature, that
woman's nature, until the Holy Spirit has a chance of
saving him or her?" That is the first difficulty to be overcome—what state of faith in Jesus Christ have I? Then
next ask yourself, "Do I believe that the Lord Jesus Christ
can take that selfish, sensual, twisted, self-satisfied nature
that is all wrong and out of order—do I believe that He
can make it perfect in the sight of God?" Oh, do let us
get back to this tremendous confidence in the Lord Jesus
Christ's power, back to reliance on the Holy Spirit, and
to remembering that Jesus came to seek the lost. WG 26

Eternal life is the gift of the Lord Jesus Christ. "He that believeth on Me hath everlasting life"(John 6:47), meaning the life He manifested in His human flesh when He was here, and says Jesus, "Ye have not (that) life in yourselves." His life is not ours by natural birth, and it can only be given to us by means of His cross. Our Lord's cross is the gateway into His life; His resurrection means that He has power now to convey that life to us. PR 111

～ 13 ～

JESUS BEGINS TO PREACH AND HEAL

READING: LUKE 4:16–30; JOHN 4:43–54
"The Spirit of the Lord is on me,
    because he has anointed me
    to preach good news to the poor.
He has sent me to proclaim freedom
    for the prisoners and recovery
    of sight for the blind,
to release the oppressed."

LUKE 4:18

To picture Jesus Christ as One who sits down beside the brokenhearted [to sympathize], is not only thoroughly to misunderstand our Lord, but to prevent Him from doing what He came to do. He does come to the brokenhearted, to the captives bound by a cursed hereditary tendency, to the blind who grope for light, to the man bruised and crushed by his surroundings, but He does not come as a sympathizer. He "binds up the brokenhearted, gives release to the captives, recovering of sight to the blind; He sets at liberty them that are bruised"

40

(Luke 4:18). Jesus Christ is not a mere sympathizer, He is a Savior, and the only One. SH 140

We *see* for the first time when we do not look. We see actual things, and we say that we see them, but we never really see them until we see God; when we see God, everything becomes different. It is not the external things that are different, but a different disposition looks through the same eyes as the result of the internal surgery that has taken place. We see God, and then we see things actually as we never saw them before. NKW 54

His Popularity Grows

∼14∼

Jesus Calls His First Disciples

Reading: Luke 5:1–11
(Supplementary reading: Matthew 4:18–22;
Mark 1:16–20)

Then Jesus said to Simon, "Don't be afraid; from now on you will catch men."

Luke 5:10

Pay attention to the source, believe in Jesus, and God will look after the outflow. God grant that we may let the Holy Ghost work out His passion for souls through us. We have not to imitate Jesus by having a passion for souls like His, but to let the Holy Ghost so identify us with Jesus that His mind is expressed through us as He expressed the mind of God. MFL 118

God grant we may understand that the passion for souls is not a placid, scientifically worked-out thing; it compresses all the energy of heart and brain and body in one consuming drive, day and night from the beginning of life to the end—a consuming, fiery, living passion. WG 82

∽15∽

Jesus Drives Out Evil Spirits and Heals Many

Reading: Luke 4:31–41
(Supplementary reading: Matthew 8:14–17;
Mark 1:21–34)

All the people were amazed and said to each other, "What is this teaching? With authority and power he gives orders to evil spirits and they come out!"

Luke 4:36

Jesus did not teach new things; He taught "as one having authority," with power to make men into accordance with what He taught. HG 57

The tendency is strong to make the statements of the Bible simpler than God makes them, the reason being that we will not recognize Jesus Christ as the authority. It is only when we rely on the Holy Spirit and obey His leadership that the authority of Jesus Christ is recognized. IWP 122

The disciple's Lord is the supreme authority in every relationship of life the disciple is in or can be in. IWP 123

∽16∽

Jesus Prays, Preaches, and Heals

Reading: Mark 1:35–45; 2:1–12
(Supplementary reading: Matthew 8:1–13;
Luke 4:42–5:26; John 5:1–15)

When Jesus saw their faith, he said to the paralytic, "Son, your sins are forgiven."

Mark 2:5

The great miracle of the grace of God is that He forgives sin, and it is the death of Jesus Christ alone that enables the divine nature to forgive and to remain true to itself in doing so. It is shallow nonsense to say that God forgives us because He is love. When we have been convicted of sin, we will never say this again. The love of God means Calvary, and nothing less; the love of God is spelled on the cross and nowhere else. The only ground on which God can forgive me is through the cross of my Lord. There, His conscience is satisfied. MUH 324

When God forgives a man, He gives him the heredity of His own Son, and there is no man on earth but can be presented "perfect in Christ Jesus." Then on the ground of the redemption, it is up to me to live as a son of God. HGM 102

THE SON GIVES LIFE

READING: JOHN 5:16–47
"I tell you the truth, whoever hears my word and believes him who sent me has eternal life and will not be condemned; he has crossed over from death to life."
JOHN 5:24

The life which Jesus Christ exhibited was eternal life, and He says anyone who believes in Him—commits himself to Him—has that life. To commit myself to Jesus means there is nothing that is not committed. Belief is a twofold transaction—a deliberate destroying of all roads back again, and a complete surrender to our Lord Himself. HG 110

"This is life eternal, that they might know Thee" (John 17:3). Eternal life is God and God is eternal life; and the meaning of the atonement is that Jesus produces that life in us. By sanctification we enter into the kingdom of perfect oneness with Jesus Christ; everything He is, we are by faith. He is "made unto us wisdom and righteousness, and sanctification, and redemption" (1 Cor. 1:30); we have nothing apart from Him. OBH 88

∼ 18 ∼

Jesus, Lord of the Sabbath

Reading: Matthew 12:1–21
(Supplementary reading: Mark 2:23–3:6; Luke 6:1–11)
"Here is my servant whom I have chosen, the one I love, in whom I delight."

Matthew 12:18

"To serve the living and true God" (1 Thess. 1:9). This means a life laid down for Jesus, a life of narrowed interests, a life that deliberately allows itself to be swamped by a crowd of paltry things. It is not fanaticism; it is the steadfast, flintlike attitude of heart and mind and body for one purpose—spoiled for everything saving as we can be used to win souls for Jesus. PS 22

You never find a saint being consciously used by God; He uses some casual thing you never thought about, which is the surest evidence that you have got beyond the stage of conscious sanctification. You are beyond all consciousness because God is taking you up into His consciousness; you are His, and life becomes the natural simple life of a child. CHI 93

∾ 19 ∾

JESUS BEGINS HIS SERMON ON THE MOUNT

READING: MATTHEW 5:1–12
(SUPPLEMENTARY READING: MARK 3:13–19;
LUKE 6:12–26)

Now when he saw the crowds, he went up on a mountainside and sat down. His disciples came to him, and he began to teach them.

MATTHEW 5:1

Wherever Christianity has ceased to be vigorous, it is because it has become Christian *ethics* instead of the Christian *evangel*. People will listen more readily to an exposition of the Sermon on the Mount than they will to the meaning of the cross, but they forget that to preach the Sermon on the Mount apart from the cross is to preach an impossibility. What is the good of telling me to love my enemies and that "Blessed are the pure in heart"? You may talk like that to further orders, but it does not amount to anything. Jesus Christ did not come to teach men to be or do any of these things: He did not come primarily to teach, He came to make a man the possessor of His own disposition, the disposition portrayed in the Sermon on the Mount. BE 66

The Sermon on the Mount is not a set of principles to be obeyed apart from identification with Jesus Christ. The Sermon on the Mount is a statement of the life we will live when the Holy Spirit is getting His way with us. PR 34

∼ 20 ∼

Salt, Light, and Oaths

Reading: Matthew 5:13–37

"You are the salt of the earth. . . . You are the light of the world."

Matthew 5:13–14

A Christian is salt, and salt is the most concentrated thing known. Salt preserves wholesomeness and prevents decay. It is a disadvantage to be salt. Think of the action of salt on a wound, and you will realize this. If you get salt into a wound, it hurts, and when God's children are among those who are "raw" towards God, their presence hurts. The man who is wrong with God is like an open wound, and when "salt" gets in it causes annoyance and distress and he is spiteful and bitter. The disciples of Jesus in the present dispensation preserve society from corruption; the "salt" causes excessive irritation which spells persecution for the saint. SSM 19

"Ye are the light of the world." We have the idea that we are going to shine in heaven, but we are to shine down here, "in the midst of a crooked and perverse nation." We are to shine as lights in the world in the squalid places, and it cannot be done by putting on a brazen smile. The light must be there all the time. LG 45

"Agree with thine adversary quickly." Have you suddenly turned a corner in any relationship and found that you had anger in your heart? Confess it quickly, quickly put it right before God, be reconciled to that one—*do it now*. MUH 182

∼21∼

AN EYE FOR AN EYE

READING: MATTHEW 5:38–6:24
(SUPPLEMENTARY READING: LUKE 6:27–36)

"But I tell you, Do not resist an evil person. If someone strikes you on the right cheek, turn to him the other also."

MATTHEW 5:39

These verses reveal the humiliation of being a Christian. Naturally, if a man does not hit back, it is because he is a coward; but spiritually if a man does not hit back, it is a manifestation of the Son of God in him. When you are insulted, you must not only not resent it, but make it an occasion to exhibit the Son of God. You cannot imitate the disposition of Jesus; it is either there or it is not. To the saint, personal insult becomes the occasion of revealing the incredible sweetness of the Lord Jesus. The teaching of the Sermon on the Mount is not, Do your duty, but, Do what is not your duty. It is not your duty to go the second mile, to turn the other cheek, but Jesus says if we are His disciples we shall always do these things. MUH 196

"Be perfect, therefore, as your heavenly Father is perfect."

MATTHEW 5:48

God always ignores the present perfection for the ultimate perfection. He is not concerned about making you blessed and happy just now; He is working out His ultimate perfection all the time, "that they may be one even as We are." MUH 118

"Store up for yourselves treasures in heaven, where moth and rust do not destroy, and where thieves do not break in and steal. For where your treasure is, there your heart will be also."

MATTHEW 6:20–21

When we lay up treasure on earth it may go at any moment, but when we learn to lay up treasure in heaven, nothing can touch it: "Therefore will not we fear, though the earth be removed . . ." (Ps. 46:2) it is perfectly secure. MFL 112

∼22∼

THE SERMON ON THE MOUNT CONCLUDED

READING: MATTHEW 6:25–7:12
(SUPPLEMENTARY READING: LUKE 6:37–42)
"Do not worry about your life, what you will eat or drink; or about your body, what you will wear."

MATTHEW 6:25

If all power is given to Jesus Christ, what right have I to insult Him by worrying? If we will let these words of Jesus come into our heart, we shall soon see how contemptible our unbelief is. Jesus Christ will do anything for us in keeping with His own character; the power that comes from Him is stamped with His nature. BSG 57

"Why do you look at the speck of sawdust in your brother's eye and pay no attention to the plank in your own eye?"

MATTHEW 7:3

It is a great education to try to put yourself into the circumstances of others before passing judgment on them. SHH 113

"Enter through the narrow gate. For wide is the gate and broad is the road that leads to destruction, and many enter through it."

MATTHEW 7:13

The freedom man has is not that of power but of choice; consequently, he is accountable for choosing the course he takes. For instance, we can choose whether or not we will accept the proposition of salvation which God puts before us; whether or not we will let God rule our lives; but we have not the power to do exactly what we like. MFL 27

The crowds were amazed at his [Jesus'] teaching, because he taught as one who had authority.

MATTHEW 7:28–29

The mainspring of the heart of Jesus Christ was the mainspring of the heart of God the Father, consequently, the words Jesus Christ spoke were the exact expression of God's thought. In our Lord the tongue was in its right place; He never spoke from His head, but always from His heart. BP 126

∼23∼

A SERVANT HEALED AND A DEAD MAN RAISED

READING: LUKE 7:1–17
(SUPPLEMENTARY READING: MATTHEW 8:5–13)

When Jesus heard this, . . . he said, "I tell you, I have not found such great faith even in Israel."

LUKE 7:9

Whenever Jesus Christ came across people who were free from the ban of finality which comes from religious beliefs, He awakened faith in them at once. The only ones who were without faith in Him were those who were bound up by religious certitude. Faith means that I commit myself to Jesus, project myself absolutely on to Him, sink or swim—and you do both; you sink out of yourself and swim into Him. Faith is implicit confidence in Jesus and in His faith. It is one thing to have faith in Jesus and another thing to have faith about everything for which He has faith. CHI 60

Our Lord did not rebuke His disciples for making mistakes, but for not having faith. The two things that astonished Him were "little faith" and "great faith." Faith is not in what Jesus Christ can do, but in Himself, and anything He can do is less than Himself. LG 150

∼ 24 ∼

JESUS ANOINTED BY A SINFUL WOMAN

READING: LUKE 7:36–50

Jesus said to the woman, "Your faith has saved you; go in peace."

LUKE 7:50

Jesus Christ did not come to fling forgiveness broadcast; He did not come to the Pharisees, who withstood Him and said He was possessed with a devil, and say,

51

"I forgive you." He said, "How can you escape the damnation of hell?" (Matt. 23:33). We may talk as much as we like about forgiveness, but it will never make any difference to us unless we realize that we need it. God can never forgive the man who does not want to be forgiven. HGM 101

When we turn to God and say we are sorry, Jesus Christ has pledged His word that we will be forgiven, but the forgiveness is not operative unless we turn, because our turning is the proof that we know we need forgiveness. HGM 104

~25~

THE SIGN OF JONAH AND DOING GOD'S WILL

READING: MATTHEW 12:38–50
(SUPPLEMENTARY READING: MARK 3:31–35; LUKE 8:19–21)
"For whoever does the will of my Father in heaven is
my brother and sister and mother."

MATTHEW 12:50

When the Spirit of God comes into a man, He brings His own generating willpower and causes him to will with God, and we have the amazing revelation that the saint's free choices are the predeterminations of God. That is a most wonderful thing in Christian psychology, that a saint chooses exactly what God predetermined he should choose. If you have never received the Spirit of God, this will be one of the things which is "foolishness" to you; but if you have received the Spirit and are obeying Him, you find He brings your spirit into complete harmony with God and the sound of your goings and the sound of God's goings are one and the same. BP 215

Surrender is not the surrender of the external life, but of the will; when that is done, all is done. There are very few crises in life; the great crisis is the surrender of the will. God never crushes a man's will into surrender; He never beseeches him; He waits until the man yields up his will to Him. MUH 257

The Parable of the Sower

READING: MATTHEW 13:1–23
(SUPPLEMENTARY READING: MARK 4:1–20; LUKE 8:4–15)
"But blessed are your eyes because they see, and your ears because they hear."

MATTHEW 13:16

If we want to know what God is like, let us study the Lord Jesus. "He that hath seen Me hath seen the Father" (John 14:9). How did people see Him in the days of His flesh? By their natural eyes? No, after His resurrection they received the Holy Spirit, and their eyes were opened and they knew Him. We do not know Him by the reasoning of our minds, but by the new life. Jesus Christ is to us the faithful face of God. PR 138

Jesus Christ continually referred to hearing: "He that hath ears to hear, let him hear" (Matt. 11:15). We say that He means the ears of our heart, but that is very misleading. He means our physical ears which are trained to hear by the disposition of our soul life. God spoke to

Jesus once and the people said it thundered, but Jesus did not think it thundered; His ears were trained by the disposition of His soul to know His Father's voice. BP 74

∼27∼

THE PARABLE OF THE WEEDS

READING: MATTHEW 13:24–43

"The Son of Man will send out his angels, and they will weed out of his kingdom everything that causes sin and all who do evil."

MATTHEW 13:41

The judgments of God leave scars, and the scars remain until I humbly and joyfully recognize that the judgments are deserved and that God is justified in them. CHI 70

There are dark and mysterious and perplexing things in life, but the prevailing authority at the back of all is a righteous authority, and a man does not need to be unduly concerned. When we do find out the judgment of God, we shall be absolutely satisfied with it to the last degree; we won't have another word to say "that Thou mightest be justified when Thou speakest, and be clear when Thou judgest." SHH 37

∼28∼

JESUS CALMS A STORM

READING: MATTHEW 8:8, 23–27
(SUPPLEMENTARY READING: MARK 4:35–41; LUKE 8:22–25)
He replied, "You of little faith, why are you so afraid?"

Then he got up and rebuked the winds and the waves, and it was completely calm.

MATTHEW 8:26

The majority of us believe in Jesus Christ only as far as we can see by our own wits. If we really believed Him, what a mighty difference there would be in us! We would trust His mind instead of our own; we would stop being "amateur providences" over other lives, and we would be fit to do our twenty-four-hours work like no else. "Except ye become as little children" (Matt. 18:3)— simple-hearted, trusting, and not being afraid. BE 49

To have faith tests a man for all he is worth. He has to stand in the commonsense universe in the midst of things which conflict with his faith, and place his confidence in the Word whose character is revealed in Jesus Christ. SSM 66

Faith must be tried or it is not faith; faith is not mathematics nor reason. Scriptural faith is not to be illustrated by the faith we exhibit in our commonsense life; it is trust in the character of One we have never seen, in the integrity of Jesus Christ, and it must be tried. PH 204

∾ 29 ∾

THE HEALING OF A DEMON-POSSESSED MAN

READING: MARK 5:1–20
(SUPPLEMENTARY READING: MATTHEW 8:28–34;
LUKE 8:26–39)

For Jesus had said to him, "Come out of this man, you evil spirit!"

MARK 5:8

The New Testament is full of the supernatural; Jesus Christ continually looked on scenery we do not see and saw supernatural forces at work. "Try the spirits whether they are of God" (1 John 4:1). The soul of man may be vastly complicated by interference from the supernatural, but Jesus Christ can guard us there. BP 91

Just as man may become identified with Jesus Christ, so he can be identified with the devil. Just as a man can be born again into the kingdom where Jesus Christ lives and moves and has His being and can become identified with Him in entire sanctification, so he can be born again, so to speak, into the devil's kingdom and be entirely consecrated to the devil. BP 92

The devil is a bully, but he cannot stand for a second before God. IYA 32

～30～

JESUS HEALS A SICK WOMAN AND RAISES A DEAD GIRL

READING: MARK 5:21–43
(SUPPLEMENTARY READING: MATTHEW 9:18–26;
LUKE 8:40–56)
He took her by the hand and said to her, *"Talitha koum!"*
(which means, "Little girl, I say to you, get up!").
MARK 5:41

Jesus Christ has destroyed the dominion of death, and He can make us fit to face every problem of life, more than conqueror all along the line. RTR 54

The Bible reveals that death is inevitable: "and so death passed upon all men" (Rom. 5:12). "It is appointed unto men once to die" (Heb. 9:27). Repeat that over to yourself. It is appointed to everyone of us that we are going to cease to be as we are now, and the place that knows us now shall know us no more. We may shirk it, we may ignore it, we may be so full of robust health and spirits that the thought of death never enters, but it is inevitable. Another thing—the Bible says that a certain class of man is totally indifferent to death, "for there are no bands [pangs] in their death" (Ps. 73:4). Over and over again the Bible points out that the wicked man, the Esau-type of man who is perfectly satisfied with life as it is, has not the slightest concern about death—because he is so brave and strong? No, because he is incapable of realizing what death means. The powers that press from the natural world have one tendency, and one only, to deaden all communication with God. SHL 25

∼ 31 ∼

A Prophet without Honor in His Hometown

READING: MATTHEW 9:27–34; 13:54–58
Jesus said to them, "Only in his hometown and in his own house is a prophet without honor."

MATTHEW 13:57

Before the Holy Spirit can materialize in the saints of this present age as He did in the prophets of old, a perfect holiness—physical, moral, and spiritual—is necessary. This is what Jesus Christ has wrought for us in the atonement, and this is what is meant by entire sanctification. On that foundation the true elements of prophecy are built. A prophet is not a sanctified gypsy telling fortunes, but one who speaks as he is moved by the Holy Spirit within. CD VOL. 2 113

The outstanding characteristic of the ancient people of God, of our Lord Jesus Christ, and of the missionary is the "prophet," or preaching, characteristic. In the Old Testament the prophet's calling is placed above that of king and of priest. It is the lives of the prophets that prefigure the Lord Jesus Christ. The character of the prophet is essential to his work. The characteristic of God's elective purpose in the finished condition of His servant is that of preaching. "It pleased God by the foolishness of preaching to save them that believe" (1 Cor. 1:21). SSY 107

∼ 32 ∼
JESUS SENDS OUT THE TWELVE

READING: MATTHEW 9:35–10:11
(SUPPLEMENTARY READING: MARK 6:6–13; LUKE 9:1–6)
"Anyone who does not take his cross and follow me is not worthy of me."

MATTHEW 10:38

The aspect of the cross in discipleship is lost altogether in the present-day view of following Jesus. The cross is looked upon as something beautiful and simple instead of stern heroism. Our Lord never said it was easy to be a Christian; He warned men that they would have to face a variety of hardships, which He termed "bearing the cross." AUG 49

The great privilege of discipleship is that I can sign on under His cross, and that means death to sin. Get alone with Jesus and either tell Him that you do not want sin to die out in you, or else tell Him that at all costs you want to be identified with His death. Immediately you transact in confident faith in what our Lord did on the cross, a supernatural identification with His death takes place, and you will know with a knowledge that passeth knowledge that your "old man" is crucified with Christ. MUH 358

What the cross was to our Lord such also in measure was it to be to those who followed Him. The cross is the pain involved in doing the will of God. AUG 51

Opposition Builds

∼33∼

Jesus Feeds the Five Thousand

Reading: John 6:1–14
(Supplementary reading: Matthew 14:13–21;
Mark 6:30–44; Luke 9:10–17)

Jesus then took the loaves, gave thanks, and distributed to those who were seated as much as they wanted. He did the same with the fish.

John 6:11

Jesus Christ represents the Bread of God broken to feed the world, and the saints are to be broken bread in His hands to satisfy Jesus Christ and His saints. . . . When by the sanctifying power of the grace of God we have been made into bread, our lives are to be offered first of all to Jesus Christ. SHL 122

The consummation of self-sacrifice is that just as our Lord was made broken bread and poured-out wine for us, so he can make us broken bread and poured-out wine for others; but He cannot do it if there is anything in us that would make us give way to self-pity when he begins to break us. The one mainspring of the life is personal, passionate devotion to Jesus Christ. SHL 123

∼34∼

JESUS WALKS ON THE WATER

READING: JOHN 6:15–24
(SUPPLEMENTARY READING: MATTHEW 14:22–36;
MARK 6:45–56)
But he said to them, "It is I; don't be afraid."
JOHN 6:20

If Jesus Christ is God, where is my trust in Him? If He is not God, why am I so foolish as to pretend to worship Him? HGM 91

Jesus Christ teaches us to build our confidence in the abiding reality of Himself in the midst of everything. If a man puts his confidence in the things which must go, imagine his incomprehensible perplexity when they do go. No wonder Jesus said, "Men's hearts failing them for fear" (Luke 21:26). These words describe the time we are in now. HGM 93

We step right out on God over some things, then self-consideration enters in and down we go. If you are recognizing your Lord, you have no business with where He engineers your circumstances. The actual things *are,* but immediately you look at them and you are overwhelmed; you cannot recognize Jesus, and the rebuke comes: "Wherefore did thou doubt?" (Matt. 14:31). Let actual circumstances be what they may; keep recognizing Jesus [and] maintain complete reliance on Him. MUH 170

～35～

JESUS, THE BREAD OF LIFE

READING: JOHN 6:25–59

"I am the living bread that came down from heaven. If anyone eats of this bread, he will live forever. This bread is my flesh, which I will give for the life of the world."

JOHN 6:51

We may talk about God as the Almighty, the All-powerful, but He means nothing to us unless He has become incarnated and touched human life where we touch it; and the revelation of redemption is that God's thought did express itself in Jesus Christ, that God became manifest on the plane on which we live. HGM 95

The Christian revelation is not that Jesus Christ stands to us as the representative of God, but that He *is* God. If He is not, then we have no God. "God was in Christ, reconciling the world unto Himself" (2 Cor. 5:19). We do not worship an austere, remote God; He is here in the thick of it. BE 61

～36～

MANY DISCIPLES DESERT JESUS

READING: JOHN 6:60–71

Simon Peter answered him, "Lord, to whom shall we go? You have the words of eternal life."

JOHN 6:68

If all Jesus came to do was to tell me I must have an unsullied career, when my past has been blasted by sin and wickedness on my own part, then He but tantalizes me. If He is simply a teacher, He only increases our capacity for misery, for He sets up standards that stagger us. But the teaching of Jesus Christ is not an ideal; it is the statement of the life we will live when we are readjusted to God by the atonement. BE 119

The teaching of Jesus Christ is very fine and delightful, but it is all up in the clouds. How are we to come up to it with our heredity, with what we are with our past, with our present, and with the outlook we have? How are we going to begin to do it if all He came to do was to teach? All attempts at imitation will end in despair, in fanaticism, and in all kinds of religious nonsense. But when once we see that the New Testament emphasizes Jesus Christ's death, not His life, that it is by virtue of His death we enter into His life, then we find that His teaching is for the life He puts in. SA 40

~37~

JESUS TEACHES ABOUT INNER PURITY

READING: MARK 7:1–23
(SUPPLEMENTARY READING: MATTHEW 15:1–20)
"For from within, out of men's hearts, come evil thoughts, . . . and make a man 'unclean.'"
MARK 7:21–23

Jesus Christ is either the supreme authority on the human heart or He is not worth listening to, and He said: "For from within, out of the heart of men, proceed" (Mark 7:21), and then comes that very ugly catalog. Jesus did not say, "Into the human heart these things are injected," but "from within, out of the heart of men" all these evil things proceed. If we trust our innocent ignorance to secure us, it is likely that as life goes on there will come a burst-up from underneath into our conscious life which will reveal to us that we are uncommonly like what Jesus Christ said. SHL 63

When God has put His Spirit in you and identified you with Jesus Christ, what is to be your attitude to your bodily life? You have the same body, the same appetites, and the same nature as before. Your members used to be servants of sin, but Jesus Christ is your example now. He sacrificed Himself to His Father's will; see that you do the same as a saint. He submitted His intelligence to His Father's will; see that you do the same as a saint. He submitted His will to His father; see that you as a saint do the same. PS 16

～38～

PETER'S CONFESSION OF CHRIST

READING: MATTHEW 16:13–28
(SUPPLEMENTARY READING: MARK 8:27–30; LUKE 9:18–27)

Simon Peter answered, "You are the Christ, the Son of the living God."

MATTHEW 16:16

"If any man will come after Me," said Jesus, the condition is that he must leave something behind—his right to himself (Matt. 16:24). Is Jesus Christ worth it, or am I one of those who accept His salvation but thoroughly object to giving up my right to myself to Him? AUG 97

"If any man would come after Me." "If" means, "You don't need to unless you like, but you won't be of any account to Me in this life unless you do." Wherever Christian experience is proving unsatisfactory, it is because the Holy Spirit is still battling around this one point—my right to myself—and until that is deliberately given over by me to Jesus Christ, I will never have the relationship to Him He asks for. HGM 140

We are apt to imagine that the cross we have to carry means the ordinary troubles and trials of life, but we must have these whether we are Christians or not. Neither is our cross suffering for conscience's sake. Our cross is something that comes only with the peculiar relationship of a disciple to Jesus Christ; it is the evidence that we have denied our right to ourselves. PR 102

∼39∼

THE TRANSFIGURATION

READING: MATTHEW 17:1–13
(SUPPLEMENTARY READING: MARK 9:2–13; LUKE 9:28–36)

"This is my Son, whom I love; with him I am well pleased. Listen to him!"

MATTHEW 17:5

If Jesus Christ had gone to heaven from the Mount of Transfiguration, He would have gone alone. He would have been to us a glorious figure, one who manifested the life of God's normal man, and how wonderful it is for God and man to live as one, but what good would that have been to us? We can never live in the power of an ideal put before us. What is the use of Jesus Christ telling us we must be as pure in heart as He is when we know we are impure? But Jesus Christ did not go to heaven from the mount. Moses and Elijah talked with Him, not of His glory, nor of His deity, but of his *death,* the issue which He was about to accomplish at Jerusalem. By His death on the cross Jesus Christ made the way for every son of man to get into communion with God. PR 119

Jesus Christ, the second Adam, the second federal head of the race, entered into this order of things as Adam did, straight from the hand of God; and He took part in His own development until it reached its climax, and He was transfigured. Earth lost its hold on Him, and He was back in the glory which He had with the Father before the world was. But He did not go to heaven from the Mount of Transfiguration because He had redemption to fulfill. He emptied Himself of His glory a second time, and came down into the world again to identify Himself with the sin of man. SA 46

∾40∾

JESUS HEALS A BOY WITH AN EVIL SPIRIT

READING: MARK 9:14–32
(SUPPLEMENTARY READING: MATTHEW 17:14–23;
LUKE 9:37–45)
"Everything is possible for him who believes."
MARK 9:23

It is a great thing to be a believer, but easy to misunderstand what the New Testament means by it. It is not that we believe Jesus Christ can *do* things, or that we believe in a plan of salvation; it is that we believe *Him;* whatever happens we will hang on to the fact that He is true. AUG 114

All the fuss and energy and work that goes on if we are not believing in Jesus Christ and His redemption has not a touch of the almighty power of God about it; it is a panic of unbelief veneered over with Christian phrases. As long as we pretend to be believers in Jesus Christ and are not, we produce humbugs, and people say, "Do you call that Christianity?" There is nothing in it, or what is worse, we produce frauds, and the worst type of fraud is religious fraud. The greatest type of reality is the Christian believer—one who has been totally readjusted on the basis of his belief. When you come across a believer in Jesus, his very presence alters your outlook. It is not that you have come to someone with amazing intelligence, but that you have come into a sanctuary which is based on a real knowledge of the redemption. HG 104

∼41∼

THE GREATEST IN THE KINGDOM OF HEAVEN

READING: MATTHEW 18:1–14
(SUPPLEMENTARY READING: MARK 9:33–50; LUKE 9:46–48)
"Therefore, whoever humbles himself like this child
is the greatest in the kingdom of heaven."
MATTHEW 18:4

Jesus Christ uses the child-spirit as a touchstone for the character of a disciple. He did not put up a child before His disciples as an ideal, but as an expression of the simple-hearted life they would live when they were born again. The life of a little child is expectant, full of wonder, and free from self-consciousness, and Jesus said, "Except ye turn, and become as little children, ye shall in no wise enter into the kingdom of heaven" (Matt. 18:3). We cannot enter into the kingdom of heaven headfirst. How many of us thought about how we should live before we were born? Why, none. But numbers of people try to think of how to live as Christians before they are born again. "Marvel not that I said unto thee, Ye must be born again" (John 3:7), that is, become as little children, with openhearted, unprejudiced minds in relation to God. There is a marvelous rejuvenescence once we let God have His way. The most seriously minded Christian is the one who has just become a Christian; the mature saint is just like a young child, absolutely simple and joyful. PH 185

The Lord Jesus spoke and worked from the great big child-heart of God. God Almighty became incarnate as a little child, and Jesus Christ's message is you must become as that, little children. IYA 43

∼42∼

DEALING WITH A BELIEVER
WHO SINS AGAINST YOU

READING: MATTHEW 18:15–20

"Again, I tell you that if two of you on earth agree about anything you ask for, it will be done for you by my Father in heaven."

MATTHEW 18:19

The revelation of our spiritual standing is what we ask in prayer; sometimes what we ask is an insult to God; we ask with our eyes on the possibilities or on ourselves, not on Jesus Christ. Get on to the supernatural line; remember that Jesus Christ is omniscient, and He says, "If ye shall ask anything in My name, I will do it" (John 14:14). BSG 58

Remember that Jesus Christ's silences are always signs that He knows we can stand a bigger revelation than we think we can. If He gives you the exact answer, He cannot trust you yet. IYA 51

～43～

THE PARABLE OF THE UNMERCIFUL SERVANT

READING: MATTHEW 18:21–35

Then Peter came to Jesus and asked, "Lord, how many times shall I forgive my brother when he sins against me? Up to seven times?"

MATTHEW 18:21

I have no right to say that I believe in forgiveness as an attribute of God if in my own heart I cherish an unforgiving temper. The forgiveness of God is the test by which I myself am judged. DI 1

When we have experienced that unfathomable forgiveness of God for all our wrong, we must exhibit that same forgiveness to others. HGM 47

Forgiveness is the divine miracle of grace. Have we ever contemplated the amazing fact that God through the death of Jesus Christ forgives us for every wrong we have ever done, not because we are sorry, but out of His sheer mercy? AUG 47

44

JESUS AT THE FEAST OF TABERNACLES

READING: JOHN 7:2–53
"He is the Christ."
JOHN 7:41

"I am . . . the first and the last" (Rev. 1:11). Is Jesus Christ the first and the last of my personal creed, the first and last of all I look to and hope for? Frequently the discipline of discipleship has to be delayed until we learn that God's barriers are put there not by sovereign deity only; they are out there by a God whose will is absolutely holy and who has told us plainly, "Not that way." IWP 126

Jesus Christ . . . can take you and me, and can fit us exactly to the expression of the divine life in us. It is not a question of putting the statements of our Lord in front of us and trying to live up to them, but of receiving His Spirit and finding that we can live up to them as He brings them to our remembrance and applies them to our circumstances. SSM 53

Jesus Christ is not only Savior; He is King, and He has the right to exact anything and everything from us at His own discretion. HGM 129

45

THE COST OF FOLLOWING JESUS

READING: MATTHEW 8:19–22; LUKE 9:57–62

Jesus replied, "No one who puts his hand to the plow and looks back is fit for service in the kingdom of God."

LUKE 9:62

Jesus Christ counts as service not what we do for Him, but what we are to Him, and the inner secret of that is identity with Him in person. "That I may know Him" (Phil. 3:10). MFL 107

Jesus Christ always talked about discipleship with an "if." We are at perfect liberty to toss our spiritual head and say, "No, thank you, that is a bit too stern for me," and the Lord will never say a word; we can do exactly what we like. He will never plead, but the opportunity is there, "If . . ." IWP 61

∼46∼

A WOMAN CAUGHT IN ADULTERY

READING: JOHN 8:1–11

"Then neither do I condemn you," Jesus declared. "Go now and leave your life of sin."

JOHN 8:11

If the redemption cannot get hold of the worst and vilest, then Jesus Christ is a fraud. But if [the Bible] means anything, it means that at the wall of the world stands God, and any man driven there by conviction of sin finds the arms of God outstretched to save him. God can forgive a man anything but despair that He can forgive him. HGM 65

There is no obstacle—nothing in the past or the present or in his heredity—that can stand in a man's way if he will only make room for Jesus Christ. Once let him

71

realize his need—"I can't be holy, I can't be pure in heart, I can't be the child of my Father in heaven and be kind to the unthankful and evil, I can't love my enemies"— Jesus Christ claims that He can do all that for him, but it depends on the man, upon how much he has come up against the things he cannot do for himself. HGM 109

When Jesus Christ says, "Sin no more," He conveys the power that enables a man not to sin anymore, and that power comes by right of what He did on the cross. That is the unspeakable wonder of the forgiveness of God. PH 184

∼47∼

JESUS, THE LIGHT OF THE WORLD

READING: JOHN 8:12–30

When Jesus spoke again to the people, he said, "I am the light of the world. Whoever follows me will never walk in darkness, but will have the light of life."

JOHN 8:12

To walk in the light means that everything that is of the darkness drives me closer into the center of the light. MUH 361

If we have entered into the heavenly places in Christ Jesus, the light has shone, and, this is the marvelous thing, as we begin to do what we know the Lord would have us do, we find He does not enable *us* to do it, He simply puts through us all His power and the thing is done in His way. Thank God for everyone who has seen the light, who has understood how the Lord Jesus Christ

clears away the darkness and brings the light by show-
ing His own characteristics through us. OBH 40

∼48∼

WHOSE CHILDREN, REALLY?

READING: JOHN 8:31–47

To the Jews who had believed him, Jesus said, "If you
hold to my teaching, you are really my disciples."

JOHN 8:31

No man begins his Christian life by believing a creed.
The man with a dogmatic creed says, "You must believe
this and that." Jesus says, "Do the will," meaning
"commit yourself to Me." Truth is not in a particular
statement; truth is a person—"I am the Truth" (John
14:6). It is a mistake to attempt to define what a man
must believe before he can be a Christian; his beliefs
are the effect of his being a Christian, not the cause of
it. [When] you lose sight of the central, majestic figure
of Jesus Christ, you are swept off your feet by all kinds
of doctrine, and when big things hit, you find your religion does not stand you in good stead because your
creed does not agree with the truth. CHI 46

Jesus does not take men and say, "This is the truth and
if you don't believe it you will be damned." He simply
shows us the truth—"I am the Truth"—and leaves us
alone. We name His name, but is He the truth to us in
our bodily life, in our commonsense life, in our intellectual and emotional life? It takes a long while for us to
begin to see that Jesus Christ is the truth. Truths exist that
have no meaning for us until we get into the domain of

their power. "Verily, verily, I say unto thee, Except a man be born anew, he cannot see the kingdom of God" (John 3:3). We want to get at truth by shortcuts; the wonder is our Lord's amazing patience. He never insists that we take His way; He simply says, "I am the Way." PH 102

∼49∼

WHAT JESUS CLAIMED ABOUT HIMSELF

READING: JOHN 8:48–59

"I tell you the truth, if anyone keeps my word, he will never see death."

JOHN 8:51

"I am Alpha and Omega, the first and the last" (Rev. 1:11). Jesus Christ is the last word on God, on sin and death, on heaven and hell; the last word on every problem that human life has to face. IWP 125

All these things lead us back to Jesus Christ—He is the Truth; He is the Honorable One; He is the Just One; He is the Pure One; He is the altogether Lovely One; He is the only One of Good Report. No matter where we start from, we will always come back to Jesus Christ. MFL 81

∼50∼

JESUS HEALS A MAN BORN BLIND

READING: JOHN 9:1–41

Jesus said, "For judgment I have come into this world, so that the blind will see and those who see will become blind."

JOHN 9:39

One of the first things Jesus Christ does is to open a man's eyes, and he sees things as they are. Until then he is not satisfied with the seeing of his eyes; he wants more, anything that is hidden he must drag to the light, and the wandering of desire is the burning waste of a man's life until he finds God. His heart lusts, his mind lusts, his eyes lust, everything in him lusts until he is related to God. It is the demand for an infinite satisfaction, and it ends in the perdition of a man's life. SHH 74

We *see* for the first time when we do not look. We see actual things, and we say that we see them, but we never really see them until we see God; when we see God, everything becomes different. It is not the external things that are different, but a different disposition looks through the same eyes as the result of the internal surgery that has taken place. We see God, and then we see things actually as we never saw them before. NKW 54

∼ 51 ∼

THE GOOD SHEPHERD AND HIS FLOCK

READING: JOHN 10:1–21

"I am the good shepherd; I know my sheep and my sheep know me . . . and I lay down my life for the sheep."

JOHN 10:14–15

He [Jesus] deliberately laid down His life without any possibility of deliverance. There was no compulsion; it was a sacrifice made with a free mind, nor was there anything of the impulsive about it. He laid down

His life with a clear knowledge of what He was doing. Jesus understood what was coming; it was not a foreboding, but a certainty; not a catastrophe which might happen, but an ordained certainty in the decrees of God, and He knew it. GW 113

Jesus Christ laid down His holy life for His Father's purposes, then if we are God's children we have to lay down our lives for His sake—not for the sake of a truth, not for the sake of devotion to a doctrine, but for Jesus Christ's sake—the personal relationship all through. IWP 85

The idea of sacrifice is giving back to God the best we have in order that He may make it His and ours forever. PR 102

～52～

JESUS SENDS OUT THE SEVENTY-TWO

READING: LUKE 10:1–24
(SUPPLEMENTARY READING MATTHEW 11:20–30)
"The harvest is plentiful, but the workers are few. Ask the Lord of the harvest, therefore, to send out workers into his harvest field."

LUKE 10:2

Concentrate on God; let Him engineer circumstances as He will, and wherever He places you He is binding up the brokenhearted through you, setting at liberty the captives through you, doing His mighty soul-saving work through you, as you keep rightly related to Him. Self-conscious service is killed, self-conscious devotion is gone, only one thing remains—"witnesses unto Me," Jesus Christ first, second, and third. MFL 108

The key to the missionary is the absolute sovereignty of the Lord Jesus Christ. We must get into real solitude with Him, feed our soul on His Word, and He will engineer our circumstances. "Consider the lilies . . . how they grow" (Matt. 6:28). They live where they are put, and we have to live where God places us. It is not the going of the feet, but the going of the life in real vital relationship to Jesus Christ. SSY 140

∼ 53 ∼

THE PARABLE OF THE GOOD SAMARITAN

READING: LUKE 10:25–37

"'Love the Lord your God with all your heart and with all your soul and with all your strength and with all your mind'; and, 'Love your neighbor as yourself.'"

LUKE 10:27

Jesus Christ teaches that if we have had a work of grace done in our hearts, we will show to our fellowmen the same love God has shown to us. BP 134

Love is the sovereign preference of my person for another person, and Jesus Christ demands that that other person be Himself. That does not mean we have no preference for anyone else, but that Jesus Christ has the sovereign preference; within that sovereign preference come all other loving preferences, down to flowers and animals. The Bible makes no distinction between divine love and human love; it speaks only of love. SSY 158

∼ 54 ∼
JESUS' TEACHING ON PRAYER

READING: LUKE 11:1–13

"For everyone who asks receives; he who seeks finds;
and to him who knocks, the door will be opened."

LUKE 11:10

How much of our praying is from the empty spaces
around our own hearts and how much from the basis
of the redemption, so that we give no thought for ourselves or for others, but only for Jesus Christ? Inartic-
ulate prayer, the impulsive prayer that looks so futile,
is the great thing God heeds more than anything else
because it is along the line of His program. HGM 80

"Your Father knoweth what things ye have need of,
before ye ask Him" (Matt 6:8). Then why ask? Very
evidently our ideas about prayer and Jesus Christ's are
not the same. Prayer to Him is not a means of getting
things from God, but in order that we may get to know
God. IYA 10

∼ 55 ∼
SIX WOES

READING: LUKE 11:37–54

"You Pharisees clean the outside of the cup and dish,
but inside you are full of greed and wickedness."

LUKE 11:39

Jesus Christ did not come to pronounce judgment; He
Himself is the judgment; whenever we come across Him
we are judged instantly. . . . One of the most remarkable

things about Jesus Christ is that although He was full of love and gentleness, yet in His presence everyone not only felt benefited, but ashamed. It is His presence that judges us; we long to meet Him, and yet we dread to. . . . It is not simply the things Jesus says to us directly, or what He does in the way of judgment particularly; it is Himself entirely, whenever He comes we are judged. HGM 42–43

If you refrain from all sorts of bad things, that is no sign that you are regenerated, much less sanctified! Not one bit of it. Scores of people who have not a spark of salvation live a cleaner life than some folks who say they are Christians. Entire sanctification is not mere outward cleanness or moral living. That is your definition, not God's. But spirituality is based on the most intense morality. Christianity is not the annulling of the Ten Commandments; to the contrary, it is a transfiguration of the will, which allows Jesus Christ to be manifested in every fiber of your being. DDL 21

56

Warnings and Encouragements

Reading: Luke 12:1–12

"I tell you, whoever acknowledges me before men, the Son of Man will also acknowledge him before the angels of God."

Luke 12:8

A man may betray Jesus Christ by speaking too many words, and he may betray Him through keeping his mouth shut. The revelation that perceives is that which recklessly states what it believes. When you stand up before your fellowmen and confess something about Jesus Christ, you feel you have no one to support you in the matter, but as you testify you begin to find the reality of your spiritual possessions, and there rushes into you the realization of a totally new life. PH 211

The disadvantage of a saint in the present order of things is that his confession of Jesus Christ is not to be in secret, but glaringly public. It would doubtless be to our advantage from the standpoint of self-realization to keep quiet, and nowadays the tendency to say "Be a Christian, live a holy life, but don't talk about it" is growing stronger. Our Lord uses in illustration the most conspicuous things known to men—salt, light, and a city set on a hill—and He says, "Be like that in your home, in your business, in your church; be conspicuously a Christian for ridicule or respect according to the mood of the people you are with." SSM 18

∼ 57 ∼

THE PARABLE OF THE RICH FOOL

READING: LUKE 12:13–21

Then he said to them, "Watch out! Be on your guard against all kinds of greed; a man's life does not consist in the abundance of his possessions."

LUKE 12:15

When Jesus Christ talked about discipleship, He indicated that a disciple must be detached from property and possessions, for if a man's life is in what he possesses, when disaster comes to his possessions, his life goes too. BFB 11

In civilized life it is the building up of possessions that is the snare—This is *my* house, *my* land; these are *my* books and *my* things. Imagine when they are touched! I am consumed with distress. Over and over again Jesus Christ drives this point home: Remember, don't have your heart in your possessions; let them come and go. SHH 63

∼ 58 ∼

DO NOT WORRY

READING: LUKE 12:22–34

Then Jesus said to his disciples: "Therefore I tell you, do not worry about your life, what you will eat; or about your body, what you will wear."

LUKE 12:22

Once [we] become worried . . . the choking of the grace of God begins. If we have really had wrought into our hearts and heads the amazing revelation which Jesus Christ gives that God is love and that we can never remember anything He will forget, then worry is impossible. . . . Notice how frequently Jesus Christ warns against worry. The "cares of this world" will produce worry, and the "lusts of other things" entering in will choke the word God has put in. BP 143

Suppose that God is the God we know Him to be when we are nearest to Him; what an impertinence worry is! Think of the unspeakable marvel of the remaining hours of this day, and think how easily we can shut God right out of His universe by the logic of our own heads, by a trick of our nerves, by remembering the way we have limited Him in the past—banish Him right out, and let the old drudging, carking care come in, until we are a disgrace to the name of Jesus. But once let the attitude be a continual "going out" in dependence on God, and the life will have an ineffable charm, which is a satisfaction to Jesus Christ. We have to learn how to "go out" of everything, out of convictions, out of creeds, out of experiences, out of everything, until so far as our faith is concerned, there is nothing between us and God. LG 150

∼ 59 ∼

JESUS TEACHES WATCHFULNESS

READING: LUKE 12:35–48

"From everyone who has been given much, much will be demanded; and from the one who has been entrusted with much, much more will be asked."

LUKE 12:48

With us, Christian service is something we do; with Jesus Christ it is not what we do *for* Him, but what we are *to* Him that He calls service. Our Lord always puts the matter of discipleship on the basis of devotion, not to a belief or a creed, but to Himself. There is no argument about it, and no compulsion, simply, "If you would be My disciple, you must be devoted to Me." PH 144

God's call is fitted to His nature, and I never hear His call until I have received His nature. When I have received His nature, then His nature and mine work together; the Son of God reveals Himself in me, and I, the natural man, serve the Son of God in ordinary ways, out of sheer downright devotion to Him. SSY 12

∼ 60 ∼

THE UNBELIEF OF THE JEWS

READING: JOHN 10:22–42

"My sheep listen to my voice; I know them, and they follow me."

JOHN 10:27

I will always hear what I listen for, and the ruling disposition of the soul determines what I listen for, just as the ruling disposition either keeps the eyes from beholding vanity or makes them behold nothing else. When Jesus Christ alters our disposition, He gives us the power to hear as He hears. BP 74

When we *hear* a thing is not necessarily when it is spoken, but when we are in a state to listen to it and to understand. Our Lord's statements seem to be so simple and gentle, and they slip unobserved into the subconscious mind. Then something happens in our circumstances, and up comes one of these words into our consciousness and we *hear* it for the first time, and it makes us reel with amazement. SSY 60

∼ 61 ∼

THE NARROW DOOR

READING: LUKE 13:22–30

"Make every effort to enter through the narrow door, because many, I tell you, will try to enter and will not be able to."

LUKE 13:24

The gospel gives access into privileges which no man can reach by any other way than the way Jesus Christ has appointed. Unsaved human nature resents this and tries to make out that Jesus Christ will bow in submissive weakness to the way it wants to go. The preaching of the gospel awakens an intense craving and an equally intense resentment. The door is opened wide by a God of holiness and love, and any and every man can enter in through that door, if he will. "I am the way" (John 14:6). Jesus Christ is the exclusive Way to the Father. IWP 127

"Behold, I stand at the door and knock" (Rev. 3:20). If it is true that no man can open the doors Jesus Christ has closed, it is also true that He never opens the door for His own incoming into the heart and life of a church or an individual. "If any man . . . open the door, I will come in to him" (Rev. 3:20). The experience into which Jesus Christ by His sovereignty can bring us is at-one-ment with God, a full-orbed, unworrying oneness with God. IWP 128

JESUS AT A PHARISEE'S HOUSE

READING: LUKE 14:1–24

"For everyone who exalts himself will be humbled, and he who humbles himself will be exalted."

LUKE 14:11

Jesus Christ presented humility as a description of what we shall be unconsciously when we have become rightly related to God and are rightly centered in Jesus Christ. BP 187

Humility is the exhibition of the Spirit of Jesus Christ and is the touchstone of saintliness. MFL 102

The way we continually talk about our own inability is an insult to the Creator. The deploring of our own incompetence is a slander against God for having overlooked us. Get into the habit of examining in the sight of God the things that sound humble before men, and you will be amazed at how staggeringly impertinent they are. MUH 335

~63~

THE COST OF DISCIPLESHIP

READING: LUKE 14:25–35

"If anyone comes to me and does not hate his father and mother, his wife and children, his brothers and sisters—yes, even his own life—he cannot be my disciple."

LUKE 14:26

Our Lord places our love for Him way beyond our love for father and mother; in fact, He uses a tremendous word. He says, "Unless you hate your father and mother, you cannot be My disciple" (Luke 14:26). The word *hate* appears to have been a stumbling block to a great number of people. It is quite conceivable that many persons may have such a slight regard for their fathers and mothers that it is nothing to separate from them; but the word *hate* shows what love we ought to have for our parents, an intense love; yet your love for [Him], says Jesus, is to be so intense that any other relationship is "hatred" in comparison when in conflict with [His] claims. GR 6/8/1911

The cross is the deliberate recognition of what my personal life is for—to be given to Jesus Christ; I have to take up that cross daily and prove that I am no longer my own. Individual independence has gone, and all that is left is personal passionate devotion to Jesus Christ through identification with His cross. SHL 79

THE PARABLE OF THE LOST SON

READING: LUKE 15:11–32
"When he came to his senses, he said, 'How many of my father's hired men have food to spare, and here I am starving to death!'"

LUKE 15:17

Repentance does not simply mean sorrow for sin. No! The prodigal son had remorse and sorrow while he fed pigs. In despair, he said, "How many hired servants of my father's have bread enough and to spare, and I perish with hunger!" (Luke 15:17). But was that repentance? Obviously not. The prodigal left the pigs and husks, and *went back* to his father. He said, "I . . . will say unto him, Father, I have sinned against heaven, and before thee, and am no more worthy to be called thy son; make me as one of thy hired servants" (Luke 15:18–19). Almost before he realized it, two strong arms of love embraced him, and the father clasped him to his bosom. That is repentance! The New Testament meaning of repentance is "going back." DDL 9

Modern ethical teaching bases everything on the power of the will, but we need to recognize also the perils of the will. The man who has achieved a moral victory by the sheer force of his will is less likely to want to become a Christian than the man who has come to the moral frontier of his own need. It is the obstinate man who makes vows, and by the very fulfillment of his vow he may increase his inability to see things from Jesus Christ's standpoint. GW 132

～65～

THE DEATH AND RESURRECTION
OF LAZARUS

READING: JOHN 11:1–54
Jesus said to her, "I am the resurrection and the life.
He who believes in me will live, even though he dies."
JOHN 11:25

We know nothing about the mystery of death apart from what Jesus Christ tells us; but blessed be the name of God, what He tells us makes us more than conquerors, so that we can shout the victory through the darkest valley of the shadow that ever a human being can go through. SHL 24

Some prayers are followed by silence because they are wrong, others because they are bigger than we can understand. Jesus stayed where He was—a positive staying, because He loved Martha and Mary. Did they get Lazarus back? They got infinitely more; they got to know the greatest truth mortal beings ever knew— that Jesus Christ is the Resurrection and the Life. It will be a wonderful moment for some of us when we stand before God and find that the prayers we clamored for in early days and imagined were never answered, have been answered in the most amazing way, and that God's silence has been the sign of the answer. IYA 49

On the Way to Jerusalem

∾66∾

Ten Healed of Leprosy

READING: LUKE 17:11–19
One of them, when he saw he was healed, came back, praising God in a loud voice.

LUKE 17:15

If we only praise when we feel like praising, it is simply an undisciplined expression; but if we deliberately go over the neck of our disinclination and offer the sacrifice of praise, we are emancipated by our very statements. PH 208

God's grace does not turn out milksops, but men and women with a strong family likeness to Jesus Christ. Thank God He does give us difficult things to do! A man's heart would burst if there were no way to show his gratitude. "I beseech you therefore, brethren," says Paul, "by the mercies of God, that ye present your bodies a living sacrifice" (Rom. 12:1). SSM 97

∾67∾

The Coming of the Kingdom of God

READING: LUKE 17:20–37
"The kingdom of God is within you."

LUKE 17:21

It may be hard for a rich man to enter the kingdom of heaven, but it is just as hard for a poor man to seek first the kingdom of God. HG 23

We must realize the frontiers of death, that there is no more chance of our entering the life of God than a mineral has of entering into the vegetable kingdom; we can only enter into the kingdom of God if God will stoop down and lift us up. That is exactly what Jesus Christ promises to do. RTR 33

∼68∼

THE PARABLE OF THE PHARISEE AND THE TAX COLLECTOR

READING: LUKE 18:9–14

"But the tax collector stood at a distance. He would not even look up to heaven, but beat his breast and said, 'God, have mercy on me, a sinner.'"

LUKE 18:13

What our Lord Jesus Christ wants us to present to Him is not our goodness, or our honesty, or our endeavor, but our real solid sin; that is all He can take. "For He hath made Him to be sin for us, who knew no sin" (2 Cor. 5:21). And what does He give in exchange for our solid sin? Great solid righteousness "that we might be made the righteousness of God in Him" (2 Cor. 5:21). But we must relinquish all pretense of being anything; we must relinquish in every way all claim to being worthy of God's consideration. That is the meaning of conviction of sin. CD VOL. 1 129

The first thing the Holy Spirit does when He comes in is to convict, not to comfort, because He has to let us know what we are like in God's sight; and then He brings the revelation that God will fill us with His own nature if we will let Him. OBH 58

~ 69 ~

THE RICH YOUNG RULER

READING: LUKE 18:18–30
(SUPPLEMENTARY READING: MATTHEW 19:16–30;
MARK 10:17–31)

When Jesus heard this, he said to him, "You still lack one thing. Sell everything you have and give to the poor, and you will have treasure in heaven. Then come, follow me."

LUKE 18:22

"Sell all that thou hast and distribute unto the poor." There is a general principle here and a particular reference. We are always in danger of taking the particular reference for the general principle and evading the general principle. The particular reference here is to selling material goods. The rich young ruler had deliberately to be destitute, deliberately to distribute, deliberately to discern where his treasure was, and to devote himself to Jesus Christ. The principle underlying it is that I must detach myself from everything I possess. SH 57

The rich young ruler had the master passion to be perfect. When he saw Jesus Christ, he wanted to be like Him. Our Lord never puts personal holiness to the fore when He calls a disciple; He puts absolute annihilation of my right to myself and identification with Himself—a relationship with Himself in which there is no other relationship. Luke 14:26, "If any man come to Me, and hate not his father, and mother . . . and his own life also, he cannot be my disciple," has nothing to do with salvation or sanctification, but with unconditional identification with Jesus Christ. Very few of us know the absolute "go" of abandonment to Jesus. MUH 272

∼70∼

THE REQUEST OF JAMES, JOHN, AND THEIR MOTHER

READING: MATTHEW 20:20–28; MARK 10:35–45
"Whoever wants to become great among you must be your servant."

MARK 10:43

Beware of anything that competes with loyalty to Jesus Christ. The greatest competitor of devotion to Jesus is service for Him. It is easier to serve than to be drunk to the dregs. The one aim of the call of God is the satisfaction of God—not a call to do something for Him. We are not sent to battle for God, but to be used by God in His battlings. MUH 18

The tendency today is to put the emphasis on service. Beware of the people who make usefulness their ground of appeal. If you make usefulness the test, then Jesus Christ was the greatest failure who ever lived. The lodestar of the saint is God Himself—not estimated usefulness. It is the work that God does through us that counts, not what we do for Him. MUH 243

God does not expect us to work *for* Him, but to work *with* Him. IYA 56

∼71∼

Zacchaeus the Tax Collector

Reading: Luke 19:1–10

"For the Son of Man came to seek and to save what was lost."

LUKE 19:10

No man can be saved by praying, by believing, by obeying, or by consecration; salvation is a free gift of God's almighty grace. We have the sneaking idea that we earn things and get into God's favor by what we do—by our praying, by our repentance. The only way we get into God's favor is by the sheer gift of His grace. GW 11

There is a difference between the way we try to appreciate the things of God and the way in which the Spirit of God teaches. We begin by trying to get fundamental conceptions of the creation and the world; why the devil is allowed; why sin exists. When the Spirit of God comes in, He does not begin by expounding any of these subjects. He begins by giving us a dose of the plague of our own heart; He begins where our vital interests lie—in the salvation of our souls. MFL 98

∼72∼

THE TRIUMPHAL ENTRY

READING: MATTHEW 21:1–11
(SUPPLEMENTARY READING: MARK 11:1–11;
LUKE 19:29–44; JOHN 12:12–19)

When Jesus entered Jerusalem, the whole city was stirred and asked, "Who is this?"

MATTHEW 21:10

In presenting Jesus Christ never present Him as a miraculous being who came down from heaven and worked miracles and who was not related to life as we are; that is not the gospel Christ. The gospel Christ is the being who came down to earth and lived our life and was possessed of a frame like ours. He became man in order to show the relationship man was to hold to God, and by His death and resurrection He can put any man into that relationship. Jesus Christ is the last word in human nature. AUG 44

What weakness! Our Lord lived thirty years in Nazareth with His brethren who did not believe on Him; He lived three years of popularity, scandal, and hatred; fascinated a dozen illiterate men who at the end of three years all forsook Him and fled; and finally He was taken by the powers that be and crucified outside the city wall. Judged from every standpoint save the standpoint of the Spirit of God, His life was a most manifest expression of weakness, and the idea would be strong to those in the pagan world who thought anything about Him that surely now He and His crazy tale were stamped out. CD VOL. 2 144

∼73∼

The Parable of the Two Sons

Reading: Matthew 21:28–32

"For John came to you to show you the way of righteousness, and you did not believe him, but the tax collectors and the prostitutes did. And even after you saw this, you did not repent and believe him."

MATTHEW 21:32

The reason people disbelieve God is not because they do not understand with their heads—we understand very few things with our heads—but because they turned their hearts in another direction. BP 144

Unbelief is the most active thing on earth; it is a fretful, worrying, questioning, annoying, self-centered spirit. To believe is to stop all this and let God work. RTR 44

It is a great thing to be a believer, but easy to misunderstand what the New Testament means by it. It is not that we believe Jesus Christ can *do* things, or that we believe in a plan of salvation; it is that we believe *Him;* whatever happens we will hang [on] to the fact that He is true. If we say, "I am going to believe He will put things right," we shall lose our confidence when we see things go wrong. AUG 114

Our Lord's word *believe* does not refer to an intellectual act, but to a moral act; with our Lord to believe means to commit. "Commit yourself to Me," and it takes a man all he is worth to believe in Jesus Christ. AUG 114

∼74∼

THE GREATEST COMMANDMENT

READING: MATTHEW 22:34–40; MARK 12:28–34
Jesus replied: "Love the Lord your God with all your heart and with all your soul and with all your mind."
MATTHEW 22:37

Love in the Bible is one; it is unique, and the human element is but one aspect of it. It is a love so mighty, so absorbing, so intense that all the mind is emancipated and entranced by God; all the heart is transfigured by the same devotion; all the soul in its living, working, waking, sleeping moments is indwelt and surrounded and enwheeled in the rest of this love. CD VOL. 2 154

It is the most ordinary business to fall in love; it is the most extraordinary business to abide there. The same thing with regard to the love of our Lord. The Holy Ghost gives us the great power to love Jesus Christ. That is not a rare experience at all; the rare experience is to get into the conception of loving Him in such a way that the whole heart and mind and soul are taken up with Him. PH 109

∼75∼

WARNING ABOUT TEACHERS OF THE LAW

READING: MATTHEW 23:1–12
(SUPPLEMENTARY READING: MARK 12:38–40; LUKE 20:45–47)
"The teachers of the law . . . do not practice what they preach."
MATTHEW 23:2–3

The one test of a teacher sent from God is that those who listen see and know Jesus Christ better than ever they did. IWP 111

If you are a teacher sent from God, your worth in God's sight is estimated by the way you enable people to see Jesus. IWP 112

If a teacher fascinates with his doctrine, his teaching never came from God. The teacher sent from God is the one who clears the way to Jesus and keeps it clear; souls forget altogether about him because the vision of Jesus is the only abiding result. When people are attracted to Jesus Christ through you, see always that you stay on God all the time, and their hearts and affections will never stop at you. IWP 112

∼76∼

THE WIDOW'S OFFERING

READING: MARK 12:41–44; LUKE 21:1–4
Calling his disciples to him, Jesus said, "I tell you the truth, this poor widow has put more into the treasury than all the others."

MARK 12:43

Much of our modern philanthropy is based on the motive of giving to the poor man because he deserves it, or because we are distressed at seeing him poor. Jesus never taught charity from those motives: He said, "Give to him that asketh thee, not because he deserves it, but because I tell you to" (see Matt. 5:43). The great motive in all giving is Jesus Christ's command. SSM 46

We never get credit spiritually for impulsive giving. If suddenly we feel we should give a shilling to a poor man, we get no credit from God for giving it; there is no virtue in it whatever. As a rule, that sort of giving is a relief to our feelings; it is not an indication of a generous character, but rather an indication of a lack of generosity. God never estimates what we give from impulse. We are given credit for what we determine in our hearts to give, for the giving that is governed by a firm determination. The Spirit of God revolutionizes our philanthropic instincts. Much of our philanthropy is simply the impulse to save ourselves an uncomfortable feeling. The Spirit of God alters all that. As saints our attitude toward giving is that we give for Jesus Christ's sake, and from no other motive. God holds us responsible for the way we use this power of voluntary choice. BP 108

~77~

Some Greeks Seek Jesus

READING: JOHN 12:20–36

"Put your trust in the light while you have it, so that you may become sons of light."

JOHN 12:36

"If therefore the light that is in thee be darkness, how great is that darkness!" (Matt. 6:23). Darkness is my own point of view; when once I allow the prejudice of my head to shut down the witness of my heart, I make my heart dark. BP 138

"If we walk in the light, as He is in the light" (1 John 1:7). Walking in the light means walking according to His standard, which is now ours. RTR 36

∽78∽

Signs of the End of the Age

Reading: Matthew 24:1–51
(Supplementary reading: Mark 13:1–37; Luke 21:5–36)

"For many will come in my name, claiming, 'I am the Christ,' and will deceive many."

MATTHEW 24:5

Today we have all kinds of christs in our midst— the christ of labor and socialism, the mind-cure christ and the christ of Christian science and theosophy— but they are all abstract christs. The one great sign of Christ is not with them—there are no marks of the atonement about these christs. Jesus Christ is the only One with the marks of atonement on Him, the wounded hands and feet, a symbol of the Redeemer who is to come again. There will be signs and wonders wrought by these other christs, and great problems may be solved, but the heartbreaking agony and long-suffering patience that they might be reconciled to His way of salvation. GW 73

To call war either diabolical or divine is nonsense; war is human. War is a conflict of wills, not something that can be solved by law or philosophy. If you take what I want, you may talk till all's blue; either I will hit you or you'll hit me. It is no use to arbitrate when you get below into the elemental. In the time between birth and death, this conflict of wills will go on until men by their relationship to God receive the disposition of the Son of God, which is holiness. SHH 28

～79～

THE PARABLE OF THE TEN VIRGINS

READING: MATTHEW 25:1–13

"But while they were on their way to buy the oil, the bridegroom arrived. The virgins who were ready went in with him to the wedding banquet. And the door was shut."

MATTHEW 25:10

What idea have you of the salvation of your soul? The experience of salvation means that in your actual life things are really altered; you no longer look at things as you used to; your desires are new; old things have lost their power. One of the touchstones of experience is, Has God altered the thing that matters? If you still hanker after the old things, it is absurd to talk about being born from above; you are juggling with yourself. If you are born again, the Spirit of God makes the alteration manifest in your actual life and reasoning, and when the crisis comes you are the most amazed person on earth at the wonderful difference there is in you. MUH 317

Nowhere does the Bible say that God holds man responsible for having the disposition of sin; but what God does hold man responsible for is refusing to let

Him deliver him from that heredity the moment he sees and understands that that is what Jesus Christ came to do. BP 228

Salvation means that if a man will turn—and every man has the power to turn, if it is only a look toward the cross, he has the power for that—if a man will but turn, he will find that Jesus is able to deliver him not only from the snare of the wrong disposition within him, but from the power of evil and wrong outside him. CHI 97

~80~

THE PARABLE OF THE TALENTS

READING: MATTHEW 25:14–30

"His master replied, 'Well done, good and faithful servant! You have been faithful with a few things; I will put you in charge of many things. Come and share your master's happiness!'"

MATTHEW 25:23

This slothful servant, who gave such a verdict about his Lord, is recognizable among men today; we have to realize that our capacity in spiritual things must be measured by God's promise, and our accountability to God by exactly the same dimensions. Jesus Christ demands that we shall allow the indwelling Holy Ghost to enable us to come up to the last limit of obedience. Unregenerated human nature can never attain the full obedience to the commands of Jesus Christ, yet He demands us to come up to His standard; and it is only by this reception of the Holy Spirit that we learn to do it.

Christianity is supernatural from beginning to end; when a man knows that the Lord Jesus Christ can enable him to fulfill to the hilt every one of His commands, by the indwelling Holy Spirit, he knows that there is not an aching abyss in His nature that Christ cannot satisfy, and not one supernatural command that He cannot reach, if he relies on the gifts that Christ has given him. God grant that we learn this marvelous secret. Only be strong and have good courage. Can earth, or hell or heaven, time or eternity, stand against the man or woman presenced with mighty divinity through the marvelous atonement of Christ? Nay, we are made conquering and to conquer until at last we hear from His lips: "Well done, good and faithful servant. . . . enter thou into the joy of thy Lord" (Matt. 25:21).GR 2/24/1910

A servant is one who, recognizing God's sovereign will, leaps to do that will of his own free choice. CD VOL. 1 30

～81～

THE SHEEP AND THE GOATS

READING: MATTHEW 25:31–46
"The King will reply, 'I tell you the truth, whatever you did for one of the least of these brothers of mine, you did for me.'"

MATTHEW 25:40

God does not transform a man's life by magic, but through the surrender of the man to Himself. The thirteenth chapter of 1 Corinthians is the description of the way love works out in actual life. To most of us love is a curiously useless word. The love Paul refers to is the sovereign preference of my person for another person, and that other person Jesus Christ. That sovereign preference works out in deliberate identification of myself with God's interests in other people, and God is interested in some strange people; He is interested in the man whom I am inclined to despise. PH 133

The best way to know whether I am recognizing myself in the fullness of sanctity is to watch how I behave toward the mean folks who come around. If I am learning to behave to them as God behaved to me in Jesus Christ, then I am all right; but if I have no time for them, it means that I am growing meaner and more selfish. Our Father is kind to the unthankful, to the mean. Now, He says, you be the same. The idea of sanctity is that we must be perfect in these relationships in life. PH 195

∼ 82 ∼

MARY ANOINTS JESUS AT BETHANY

READING: MATTHEW 26:6–13
(SUPPLEMENTARY READING: MARK 14:3–9; JOHN 12:2–8)
Aware of this, Jesus said to them, "Why are you bothering this woman? She has done a beautiful thing to me."
MATTHEW 26:10

There are times when it seems as if God watches to see if we will give Him the abandoned tokens of how genuinely we do love Him. Abandon to God is of more value than personal holiness. Personal holiness focuses the eye on our own whiteness; we are greatly concerned about the way we walk and talk and look, fearful lest we offend Him. Perfect love casts out all that when once we are abandoned to God. We have to get rid of this notion, "Am I of any use?" and make up our minds that we are not, and we may be near the truth. It is never a question of being of use, but of being of value to God Himself. When we are abandoned to God, He works through us all the time. MUH 52

The reason some of us are such poor specimens of Christianity is because we have no Almighty Christ. We have Christian attributes and experiences, but there is no abandonment to Jesus Christ. MUH 58

The Passion and Resurrection

∼83∼

Jesus Washes His Disciples' Feet

Reading: John 13:1–20
(Supplementary reading: Matthew 26:17–19;
Mark 14:12–17; Luke 22:7–13)

"I tell you the truth, no servant is greater than his master, nor is a messenger greater than the one who sent him."

John 13:16

We are here with no right to ourselves, for no spiritual blessing for ourselves; we are here for one purpose only—to be made servants of God as Jesus was. PS 17

The things that Jesus did were of the most menial and commonplace order, and this is an indication that it takes all God's power in me to do the most commonplace things in His way. Can I use a towel as He did? Towels and dishes and sandals—all the ordinary sordid things of our lives—reveal more quickly than anything what we are made of. It takes God Almighty incarnate in us to do the meanest duty as it ought to be done.

"I have given you an example, that ye should do as I have done to you" (John 13:15). Watch the kind of people God brings around you, and you will be humiliated to find that this is His way of revealing to you the kind of person you have been to Him. Now, He says, exhibit to that one exactly what I have shown to you. MUH 255

∼84∼

THE LAST SUPPER

READING: MATTHEW 26:26–29
(SUPPLEMENTARY READING: MARK 14:22–25;
LUKE 22:17–20; 1 CORINTHIANS 11:24–25)
"This is my blood of the covenant, which is poured out for many for the forgiveness of sins."
MATTHEW 26:28

When Jesus Christ shed His blood on the cross, it was not the blood of a martyr, or the blood of one man for another; it was the life of God poured out to redeem the world. BE 60

God redeemed the world by shedding His blood, by putting the whole passion of the Godhead into it. He did not become interested and put one arm in to help the human race up; He went into the redemption absolutely; there was nothing of Himself left out. BE 63

∼85∼

JESUS COMFORTS HIS TROUBLED DISCIPLES

READING: JOHN 14:1–14
Jesus answered, "I am the way and the truth and the life. No one comes to the Father except through me."
JOHN 14:6

However far we may drift, we must always come back to these words of our Lord: "I am the way"—

not a road that we leave behind us, but the way itself. Jesus Christ is the way *of* God, not a way that leads *to* God; that is why He says, "Come unto Me"; "abide in Me"; "I am the truth," not the truth about God, not a set of principles, but the truth itself. Jesus Christ is the truth *of* God. "No man cometh unto the Father, but by Me." We can get to God as Creator in other ways, but no man can come to God as Father in any other way than by Jesus Christ. "I am the life." Jesus Christ is the life *of* God as He is the way and the truth of God. Eternal life is not a gift *from* God; it is the gift of *God Himself*. The life imparted to me by Jesus is the life of God. "He that hath the Son hath life" (1 John 5:12); "I am come that they might have life" (John 10:10); "And this is life eternal, that they should know thee the only true God" (John 17:3). We have to abide in the *way;* to be incorporated into the *truth;* to be infused by the *life.* SSY 92

～86～

JESUS PROMISES THE HOLY SPIRIT

READING: JOHN 14:15–31
"But the Counselor, the Holy Spirit, whom the Father will send in my name, will teach you all things and will remind you of everything I have said to you."
JOHN 14:26

The thought is unspeakably full of glory, that God the Holy Ghost can come into my heart and fill it so full that the life of God will manifest itself all through this body which used to manifest exactly the opposite.

If I am willing and determined to keep in the light and obey the Spirit, then the characteristics of the indwelling Christ will manifest themselves. BP 146

The great thing that the Holy Spirit reveals is that the supernatural power of God is ours through Jesus Christ, and if we will receive the Holy Spirit He will teach us how to think as well as how to live. BE 97

~ 87 ~

THE VINE AND THE BRANCHES

READING: JOHN 15:1–17

"I am the vine; you are the branches. If a man remains in me and I in him, he will bear much fruit; apart from me you can do nothing."

JOHN 15:5

Think of the things that take you out of abiding in Christ—"Yes, Lord, just a minute, I have got this to do"; Yes, I will abide when once this is finished; when this week is over, it will be all right; I will abide then. Get a move on; begin to abide *now*. In the initial stages it is a continual effort until it becomes so much the law of life that you abide in Him unconsciously. Determine to abide in Jesus wherever you are placed. MUH 166

The secret of bringing forth fruit is to abide in Jesus. "Abide in Me," says Jesus, in spiritual matters, in intellectual matters, in money matters, in every one of the matters that make human life what it is. OBH 107

∼ 88 ∼

THE WORK OF THE HOLY SPIRIT

READING: JOHN 16:5–15

"But when he, the Spirit of truth, comes, he will guide you into all truth. He will not speak on his own; he will speak only what he hears, and he will tell you what is yet to come."

JOHN 16:13

We can only discern the spiritual world by the Spirit of God, not by our own spirit; and if we have not received the Spirit of God, we shall never discern spiritual things or understand them. We shall move continually in a dark world, and come slowly to the conclusion that the New Testament language is very exaggerated. But when we have received the Spirit of God, we begin to "know the things that are freely given to us of God," and to compare "spiritual things with spiritual," "not in the words which man's wisdom teaches, but which the Holy Ghost teaches" (1 Cor. 2:12–13). BP 210

Our great need is to ask for and receive the Holy Ghost in simple faith in the marvelous atonement of Jesus Christ, and He will turn us into passionate lovers of the Lord. It is this passion for Christ worked out in us that makes us witnesses to Jesus wherever we are, men and women in whom He delights, upon whom He can look down with approval; men and women whom He can put in the shadow or the sun; men and women whom He can put upon their beds or on their feet; men and women whom He can send anywhere He chooses. PH 33

~ 89 ~

Jesus Prays for Himself and All Believers

Reading: John 17:1–26
"They are not of the world, even as I am not of it.
Sanctify them by the truth; your word is truth."
John 17:16–17

Sanctification is the impartation to us of the holy qualities of Jesus Christ. It is His patience, His love, His holiness, His faith, His purity, His godliness that are manifested in and through every sanctified soul. The presentation [is an error] that God by sanctification plants within us His Spirit, and then setting Jesus Christ before us says, "There is your example; follow Him and I will help you, but you must do your best to follow Him and do what He did." . . . It is not true to experience, and thank God, it is not true to the wonderful gospel of the grace of God. The mystery of sanctification is "Christ in you, the hope of glory" (Col. 1:27). OBH 31

The test of sanctification is not our talk about holiness and singing pious hymns; but, what are we like where no one sees us? with those who know us best? DI 60

~ 90 ~

Gethsemane

Reading: Matthew 26:36–46
(Supplementary reading: Mark 14:32–42;
Luke 22:39–46)
Going a little farther, he fell with his face to the

ground and prayed, "My Father, if it is possible, may this cup be taken from me. Yet not as I will, but as you will."

Matthew 26:39

In the temptation of our Lord, Satan's first attack was in the physical domain. In Gethsemane his onslaught is against our Lord as Son of Man, not against Him as Son of God. Satan could not touch Him as Son of God; he could only touch Him as Son of Man, and this is his final onslaught on the Son of God as Son of Man. "You will get through as Son of God; I cannot touch You there, but You will never get one member of the human race through with You. Look at Your disciples; they are asleep [and] they cannot even watch with You. When You come to the cross, Your body will be so tortured and fatigued, so paralyzed with pain, and Your soul will be so darkened and confused, that You will not be able to retain a clear understanding of what You are doing. Your whole personality will be so clouded and crushed by the weight of sin that You will never get through as man."

If Satan had been right, all that would have happened on the cross would have been the death of a martyr only; the way into life for us would never have been opened. But if Jesus Christ does get through as Son of Man, it means that the way is open for everyone who has been born or ever will be born to get back to God. Satan's challenge to our Lord was that he would not be able to do it; He would only get through as Son of God, because

Satan could not touch Him there. The fear that came upon the Lord was that He might die before He reached the cross. He feared that as Son of Man He might die before He had opened the gate for us to get through, and He "was heard in that He feared" (Heb. 5:7), and was delivered from death in Gethsemane. PR 87

∼91∼

JESUS ARRESTED

READING: LUKE 22:47–54
(SUPPLEMENTARY READING: MATTHEW 26:47–56;
MARK 14:43–52; JOHN 18:2–11)
And he touched the man's ear and healed him.
LUKE 22:51

If you get off on the line of personal holiness or divine healing or the second coming of our Lord, and make any of these your end, you are disloyal to Jesus Christ. Supposing the Lord has healed your body and you make divine healing your end, the dead set of your life is no longer for God but for what you are pleased to call the manifestation of God in your life. Bother your life! "It can never be God's will that I should be sick." If it was God's will to bruise His own Son, why should it not be His will to bruise you! The thing that tells is not relevant consistency to an idea of what a saint's life is, but abandonment abjectly to Jesus Christ whether you are well or ill. NKW 148

When people come to the atonement and say, "Now I have deliverance in the atonement, therefore I have no business to be sick," they make a fundamental confusion, because there is no case of healing in the Bible that did not come from a direct intervention of the sovereign touch of God. IYA 85

∼92∼

PETER'S THREE DENIALS

READING: MATTHEW 26:57–75
(SUPPLEMENTARY READING: MARK 14:54–72;
LUKE 22:54–62; JOHN 18:15–27)

Then Peter remembered the word Jesus had spoken: "Before the rooster crows, you will disown me three times." And he went outside and wept bitterly.

MATTHEW 26:75

Repentance is the experimental side of redemption and is altogether different from remorse or reformation. Repentance is a New Testament word and cannot be applied outside the New Testament. We all experience remorse, disgust with ourselves over the wrong we have done when we are found out by it, but the rarest miracle of God's grace is the sorrow that puts an end forever to the thing for which I am sorry. Repentance involves the receiving of a totally new disposition so that I never do the wrong thing again. CIII 26

Strictly speaking, repentance is a gift of God. No man can repent when he chooses. A man can be remorseful when he chooses, but remorse is a lesser thing than repentance. Repentance means that I show my sorrow for the wrong thing by becoming the opposite. BFB 108

~93~

JESUS SENTENCED TO BE CRUCIFIED

READING: JOHN 19:1–27
(SUPPLEMENTARY READING: MATTHEW 27:24–44;
MARK 15:15–32; LUKE 23:23–43)

Here they crucified him, and with him two others—one on each side and Jesus in the middle.

JOHN 19:18

In the cross we may see the dimensions of divine love. The cross is not the cross of a man, but the exhibition of the heart of God. At the back of the wall of the world stands God with His arms outstretched, and every man driven there is driven into the arms of God. The cross of Jesus is the supreme evidence of the love of God. PH 65

There is nothing more certain in time or eternity than what Jesus Christ did on the cross: He switched the whole human race back into right relationship to God and made the basis of human life redemptive; consequently any member of the human race can get into touch with God *now*. BE 61

~94~

THE DEATH OF JESUS

READING: JOHN 19:28–34
(SUPPLEMENTARY READING: MATTHEW 27:45–56;
MARK 15:33–41; LUKE 23:44–49)

When he had received the drink, Jesus said, "It is finished." With that, he bowed his head and gave up his spirit.

JOHN 19:30

When we tell God that we want at all costs to be identified with the death of Jesus Christ, at that instant a supernatural identification with His death takes place, and we know with a knowledge that passes knowledge that our "old man" is crucified with Christ, and we prove it forever after by the amazing ease with which the supernatural life of God enables us to do His will. That is why the bedrock of Christianity is personal, passionate devotion to the Lord Jesus. PH 164

When we speak of the blood of Jesus Christ cleansing us from all sin, we do not mean the physical blood shed on Calvary, but the whole life of the Son of God which was poured out to redeem the world. All the perfections of the essential nature of God were in that blood, and all the holiest attainments of mankind as well. It was the life of the perfection of deity that was poured out on Calvary, ". . . the church of God, which He purchased with His own blood" (Acts 20:28). We are apt to look upon the blood of Jesus Christ as a magic-working power instead of its being the very life of the Son of God poured forth for men. The whole meaning of our being identified with the death of Jesus is that His blood may flow through our mortal bodies. PH 162

∼95∼
The Burial of Jesus

Reading: Matthew 27:57–66
(Supplementary reading: Mark 15:42–47;
Luke 23:50–56; John 19:38–42)

115

Joseph took the body, wrapped it in a clean linen cloth, and placed it in his own new tomb that he had cut out of the rock.

MATTHEW 27:59–60

The death of Jesus Christ is the performance in history of the very mind of God. There is no room for looking on Jesus Christ as a martyr; His death was not something that happened to Him which might have been prevented: His death was the very reason why He came. MUH 326

By the death of the Son of Man upon the cross, the door is opened for any individual to go straight into the presence of God; and by the resurrection our Lord can impart to us His own life. PR 111

~96~

THE RESURRECTION

READING: LUKE 24:1–12
(SUPPLEMENTARY READING: MATTHEW 28:1–8;
MARK 16:1–8; JOHN 20:1–9)
"He is not here; he has risen!"
LUKE 24:6

Our Lord died and was buried and He rose again, and this is the declaration of the resurrection in all its incredibleness. Any question that arises in connection with the resurrection arises in the minds of those who do not accept the necessity of being born from above. PR 110

The resurrection of Jesus Christ grants Him the right to give His own destiny to any human being—to make us the sons and daughters of God. His resurrection means that we are raised to His risen life, not to our old life. "Like as Christ was raised up from the dead by the glory of the Father, even so we also should walk in newness of life. . . . We shall be also in the likeness of His resurrection" (Rom. 6:4–5). PR 114

∽97∼

JESUS APPEARS TO MARY MAGDALENE AND OTHER WOMEN

READING: JOHN 20:10–18
(SUPPLEMENTARY READING: MATTHEW 28:9–15;
MARK 16:9–11; JOHN 20:10–18)

Jesus said, "Do not hold on to me, for I have not yet returned to the Father. Go instead to my brothers and tell them, 'I am returning to my Father and your Father, to my God and your God.'"

JOHN 20:17

Our Lord's cross is the gateway into His life: His resurrection means that He has the power now to convey His life to me. When I am born again from above, I receive from the risen Lord His very life.

Our Lord's resurrection destiny is to bring "many sons unto glory" (Heb. 2:10). The fulfilling of His destiny gives Him the right to make us sons and daughters of God. We are never in the relationship to God that the Son of God is in; but we are brought by the Son into the relation of sonship. When our Lord rose from the dead, He rose to an absolutely new life, to a life He did not live before He was incarnate. He rose to a life that had never been before; and His resurrection means for us

117

that we are raised to His risen life, not to our old life. One day we shall have a body like unto His glorious body, but we can know now the efficacy of His resurrection and walk in newness of life. I would know Him in the power of His resurrection (see Phil. 3:10). MUH 99

The ascension placed Jesus Christ back in the glory which He had with the Father before the world was. The ascension, not the resurrection, is the completion of the transfiguration. BSG 56

~98~

ON THE ROAD TO EMMAUS

READING: MARK 16:12–13; LUKE 24:13–35
He said to them, "How foolish you are, and how slow
of heart to believe all that the prophets have spoken!"
LUKE 24:25

How did Jesus Christ deal with the foolishness of the two disciples on the road to Emmaus? This is the stupidity on another line: a stupidity of simple souls, honest and true, who had become blinded by their own grief and their own point of view.

Jesus said to them: "O fools, and slow of heart to believe all that the prophets have spoken" (Luke 24:25). Here the word *fools* might be translated "My little children, when will you believe what the prophets have written?" This is stupidity of a totally different order—a stupidity that Jesus deals with very pointedly, but very patiently. It is a stupidity that obliterates one's understanding of the Word of God because of personal grief, sorrow, or perplexity.

Is Jesus Christ saying to you, "My child, when will you believe what I say?" Is there a particular problem in your life that has made you slow of heart to believe? Do not let the stupidity grow. Seek what the Word of God has to say about it.

Oh, there is such a need for people who will search the Bible and learn what God is saying to them! DDL 195

∽99∽

JESUS APPEARS TO HIS DISCIPLES

READING: LUKE 24:36–43; JOHN 20:19–29
Then Jesus told him, "Because you have seen me, you have believed; blessed are those who have not seen and yet have believed."

JOHN 20:29

Seeing is never believing: We interpret what we see in the light of what we believe. Faith is confidence in God before you see God emerging; therefore the nature of faith is that it must be tried. To say "Oh, yes, I believe God will triumph" may be so much credence smeared over with religious phraseology; but when you are up against things it is quite another matter to say, "I believe God will win through." The trial of our faith gives us a good banking account in the heavenly places, and when the next trial comes our wealth there will tide us over. If we have confidence in God beyond the actual earthly horizons, we shall see the lie at the heart of the fear, and our faith will win through in every detail. Jesus said that men ought always to pray and not "cave in": "Don't look at the immediate horizon and don't take the facts you see and say they are the reality; they are actuality; the reality lies behind with God." SHH 55

Belief must be the *will* to believe. There must be a surrender of the will, not a surrender to persuasive power, a deliberate launching forth on God and on what He says until I am no longer confident in what I have done; I am confident only in God. The hindrance is that I will not trust God, but only my mental understanding. As far as feelings go, I must stake all blindly. I must *will* to believe, and this can never be done without a violent effort on my part to disassociate myself from my old ways of looking at things, and by putting myself right over on to Him. MUH 357

∼ 100 ∼

THE MIRACULOUS CATCH OF FISH

READING: JOHN 21:1–23

"Feed my lambs. . . . Take care of my sheep. . . . Follow me!"

JOHN 21:15–16, 19

Jesus did not say, "Make converts to your way of thinking, but look after My sheep; see that they get nourished in the knowledge of Me." We count as service what we do in the way of Christian work; Jesus Christ calls service what we are to Him, not what we do for Him. Discipleship is based on devotion to Jesus Christ, not on adherence to a belief or a creed. "If any man come to Me and hate not . . . he cannot be My disciple" (Luke 14:26). There is no argument and no compulsion, but simply, "If you would be My disciple,

120

you must be devoted to Me." A man touched by the Spirit of God suddenly says, "Now I see who Jesus is," and that is the source of devotion.

Today we have substituted credal belief for personal belief, and that is why so many are devoted to causes and so few devoted to Jesus Christ. MUH 171

When our Lord commissioned Peter, He did not tell him to go and save souls, but, "Feed My sheep; tend My lambs; guard My flock." We have to be careful lest we rebel against the commission to disciple men to Jesus and become energetic proselytizers to our own way of thinking—"but the shepherds fed themselves, and fed not My sheep" (Ezek. 34:8). When we stand before God will He say, "Well done, good and faithful servant"? (Matt. 25:21) or will He say, "You have not been a shepherd of My sheep; you have fed them for your own interest, exploited them for your own creed"? When a soul gets within sight of Jesus Christ, leave him alone. SHH 107

∼ 101 ∼

THE GREAT COMMISSION

READING: MATTHEW 28:16–20; ACTS 1:1–12
(SUPPLEMENTARY READING: MARK 16:15–20;
LUKE 24:44–53; JOHN 20:30–31; 21:25)
"But you will receive power when the Holy Spirit comes on you; and you will be my witnesses in Jerusalem, and in all Judea and Samaria, and to the ends of the earth."

ACTS 1:8

The basis of missionary appeals is the authority of Jesus Christ, not the needs of the heathen. We are apt to look upon our Lord as One who assists us in our enterprises for God. Our Lord puts Himself as the absolute sovereign supreme Lord over His disciples. He does not say the heathen will be lost if we do not go; He simply says, "Go ye therefore and teach all nations" (Matt. 28:19). Go on the revelation of My sovereignty; teach and preach out of a living experience of Me. MUH 288

By His ascension our Lord raises Himself to glory; He becomes omnipotent, omniscient, and omnipresent. All the splendid power, so circumscribed in His earthly life, becomes omnipotence; all the wisdom and insight, so precious but so limited during His life on earth, becomes omniscience; all the unspeakable comfort of the presence of Jesus, so confined to a few in His earthly life, becomes omnipresence; He is with us all the days. SHH 189

∼ PART 2 ∼
THE EPISTLES

Romans: Justified by Faith

∼ 102 ∼

The Just Shall Live by Faith

Reading: Romans 1

I am not ashamed of the gospel, because it is the power of God for the salvation of everyone who believes: first for the Jew, then for the Gentile.

Romans 1:16

"Yea, woe is unto me, if I preach not the Gospel!" (1 Cor. 9:16). An orator rouses human nature to do what it is asleep over; the New Testament preacher has to move men to do what they are dead-set against doing—giving up the right to themselves to Jesus Christ. Consequently, the preaching of the gospel awakens a terrific longing, but an equally intense resentment. The aspect of the gospel that awakens desire in a man is the message of peace and goodwill—but I must give up my right to myself to get there. The basis of human life has been put on redemption, and on the ground of that redemption any man can be lifted into right relationship with God. The gospel is "the power of God unto salvation to everyone that believeth." There is no room for despair on the part of any man if he will only believe what the New Testament preacher proclaims—but it takes some believing. No thinking will ever make me a Christian; I can become a Christian only through listening to what is preached and accepting salvation as a gift; but I must think after I am a Christian. BE 52

～ 103 ～

GOD'S RIGHTEOUS JUDGMENT

READING: ROMANS 2

Or do you show contempt for the riches of his kindness, tolerance and patience, not realizing that God's kindness leads you toward repentance?

ROMANS 2:4

Because a man has altered his life, it does not necessarily mean that he has repented. A man may have lived a bad life and suddenly stops being bad—not because he has repented—but because he is like an exhausted volcano. The fact that he has become good is no sign of his having become a Christian. BFB 103

It is not repentance that saves me; repentance is the sign that I realize what God has done in Christ Jesus. The danger is to put the emphasis on the effect instead of on the cause: It is my obedience that puts me right with God, my consecration. Never! I am put right with God because prior to all, Christ died. When I turn to God and by belief accept what God reveals, instantly the stupendous atonement of Jesus Christ rushes me into a right relationship with God; and by the supernatural miracle of God's grace I stand justified, not because I am sorry for my sin, not because I have repented, but because of what Jesus has done. The Spirit of God brings it with a breaking, all-over light, and I know, though I do not know how, that I am saved. MUH 302

∼104∼

Made Righteous by Faith

Reading: Romans 3

No one will be declared righteous . . . by observing the law; rather, through the law we become conscious of sin. But now a righteousness from God, apart from law, has been made known. . . . This righteousness from God comes through faith in Jesus Christ.

Romans 3:20–22

Imputed righteousness must never be made to mean that God puts the robe of His righteousness over our moral wrong, like a snowdrift over a rubbish heap; that He pretends we are all right when we are not. The revelation is that Christ Jesus is made unto us righteousness (see 2 Cor. 5:21); it is the distinct impartation of the very life of Jesus on the ground of the atonement, enabling me to walk in the light as God is in the light, and as long as I remain in the light, God sees only the perfections of His Son. We are "accepted in the Beloved" (Eph. 1:6). CHI 81

No one is ever united with Jesus Christ until he is willing to relinquish not sin only, but his whole way of looking at things. To be born from above of the Spirit of God means that we must let go before we lay hold, and in the first stages it is the relinquishing of all pretense. What our Lord wants us to present to

Him is not goodness, not honesty, nor endeavor, but real solid sin; that is all He can take from us. And what does He give in exchange for our sin? Real solid righteousness. But we must relinquish all pretense of being anything, all claim of being worthy of God's consideration. MUH 68

～ 105 ～

Justification by Faith

Reading: Romans 4

He was delivered over to death for our sins and was raised to life for our justification.

ROMANS 4:25

True justification can only result in sanctification. By justification God anticipates that we are holy in His sight, and if we will obey the Holy Spirit we will prove in our actual lives that God is justified in justifying us. Ask yourself, Is God justified in my justification? Do I prove by the way I live and talk and do my work that God has made me holy? Am I converting God's purpose in justifying me into actual experience, or only delighting in God's anticipation? There is a great snare, especially in evangelical circles, of knowing the will of God as expressed in the Bible without the slightest practical working of it out in life. The Christian religion is the most practical thing on earth. CHI 58

～ 106 ～

Peace and Joy through Christ

Reading: Romans 5

Therefore, since we have been justified through faith, we have peace with God through our Lord Jesus Christ.

ROMANS 5:1

Purity in God's children is not the outcome of obedience to His Law, but the result of the supernatural work of His grace. "*I* will cleanse you"; "*I* will give you a new heart"; "*I* will put My Spirit within you, and cause you to walk in My statutes"; "*I* will do it all." GW 75

The surest sign that God has done a work of grace in my heart is that I love Jesus Christ best, not weakly and faintly, not intellectually, but passionately, personally, and devotedly, overwhelming every other love of my life. BP 134

∽ 107 ∽
DEAD TO SIN, ALIVE IN CHRIST

READING: ROMANS 6

For we know that our old self was crucified with him so that the body of sin might be done away with, that we should no longer be slaves to sin.

ROMANS 6:6

Sin is the outcome of a relationship set up between man and the devil whereby man becomes "boss" over himself, his own god. BE 52

Sin is not wrong doing; it is wrong being, independence from God. God has undertaken the responsibility for its removal on the ground of the redemption. BE 62

129

Knowledge of what sin is is in inverse ratio to its presence; only as sin goes do you realize what it is. When it is present, you do not realize what it is because the nature of sin is that it destroys the capacity to know that you sin. BE 78

∼108∼

AN ILLUSTRATION FROM MARRIAGE

READING: ROMANS 7

What a wretched man I am! Who will rescue me from this body of death? Thanks be to God—through Jesus Christ our Lord! So then, I myself in my mind am a slave to God's law, but in the sinful nature a slave to the law of sin.

ROMANS 7:24–25

The Bible reveals that death is inevitable—"and so death passed upon all men" (Rom. 5:12). "It is appointed unto men once to die" (Heb. 9:27). Repeat that over to yourself. It is appointed to every one of us that we are going to cease to be as we are now, and the place that knows us now shall know us no more. We may shirk it, we may ignore it, we may be so full of robust health and spirits that the thought of death never enters, but it is inevitable. SHL 35

The Bible says there are those who are intimidated by death, "That through death He might bring to nought him that had the power of death, that is, the devil; and might deliver them who through fear of death were all their lifetime subject to bondage" (Heb.

2:14–15). The thought of death is never away from them; it terrorizes their days, it alarms their nights. Now read very reverently Hebrews 5:7: "Who . . . had offered up prayers and supplications with strong crying and tears unto Him that was able to save Him from death." Who is that? The Lord Jesus Christ. SHL 25

～109～

LIVING IN AGREEMENT WITH THE SPIRIT

READING: ROMANS 8

Those who live according to the sinful nature have their minds set on what that nature desires; but those who live in accordance with the Spirit have their minds set on what the Spirit desires.

ROMANS 8:5

The Holy Spirit alone makes Jesus real; the Holy Spirit alone expounds His cross; the Holy Spirit alone convicts of sin; the Holy Spirit alone does in us what Jesus did for us. BE 99

When the Holy Spirit comes in, unbelief is turned out and the energy of God is put into us, and we are enabled to will and to do of His good pleasure. When the Holy Spirit comes in, He sheds abroad the love of God in our hearts, so that we are able to show our fellows the same love that God has shown to us. When the Holy Spirit comes in, He makes us as "light," and our righteousness will exceed the righteousness of the most moral, upright, natural man because the supernatural has been made natural in us. BP 222

∼ 110 ∼

ISRAEL NEEDS THE GOSPEL

READING: ROMANS 9–10

If you confess with your mouth, "Jesus is Lord," and believe in your heart that God raised him from the dead, you will be saved.

ROMANS 10:9

No man can be saved by praying, by believing, by obeying, or by consecration; salvation is a free gift of God's almighty grace. We have the sneaking idea that we earn things and get into God's favor by what we do—by our praying, by our repentance; the only way we get into God's favor is by the sheer gift of His grace. GW 11

There is nothing so secure as the salvation of God; it is as eternal as the mountains, and it is our trust in God that brings us the conscious realization of this. HG 28

∼ 111 ∼

NOT A TOTAL REJECTION

READING: ROMANS 11

Did God reject his people? By no means! . . . There is a remnant chosen by grace.

ROMANS 11:1, 5

There were no nations until after the flood. After the flood the human race was split up into nations, and God called off one stream of the human race in Abraham, and created a nation out of that one man.

The Old Testament is not a history of the nations of the world, but the history of that one nation. In secular history Israel is disregarded as being merely a miserable horde of slaves, and justly so from the standpoint of the historian. The nations to which the Bible pays little attention are much finer to read about, but they have no importance in the redemptive purpose of God. His purpose was the creation of a nation to be His bondslave, that through that nation all the other nations should come to know Him.

The idea that Israel was a magnificently developed type of nation is a mistaken one. Israel was a despised and a despisable nation, continually turning away from God into idolatry; but nothing ever altered the purpose of God for the nation. The despised element is always a noticeable element in the purpose of God. When the Savior of the world came, He came of that despised nation; He Himself was "despised and rejected of men" (Isa. 53:3), and in all Christian enterprise there is this same despised element, "things that are despised hath God chosen" (1 Cor. 1:28). SSY 104

≈ 112 ≈

LIVING SACRIFICES TO GOD

READING: ROMANS 12–13

Therefore, I urge you, brothers, in view of God's mercy, to offer your bodies as living sacrifices, holy and pleasing to God—this is your spiritual act of worship.

ROMANS 12:1

Do you understand what you have to put on the altar before you are sanctified? Your whole body, your whole soul, and your whole spirit. Why people who claim to be Christians have to be preached to about smoking and chewing tobacco and all these sorts of things is to me an amazement. There is a big mistake somewhere, and it is either in you or God, and I would rather make out man a liar and God be true, especially when I know what He has done for me. Bless my soul, if you stop all these things that is no sign that you are regenerated, much less sanctified! Not one bit of it. Scores of people who have not a spark of salvation live a cleaner life than some folks who say they are sanctified. Entire sanctification is not mere outward cleanness or moral living. That is your definition, not God's. Spirituality is based on the intensest morality. Christianity is not the annulling of the Ten Commandments. It is a transfiguration of the will. Why cannot you let God get you where Jesus Christ can be manifested in your flesh, in every fiber of your being? Jesus walking through your feet, talking through your mouth, and soothing with your hands. GR 4/30/1908

∼II3∼

Do What Leads to Peace

READING: ROMANS 14

For the kingdom of God is not a matter of eating and drinking, but of righteousness, peace and joy in the Holy Spirit.

ROMANS 14:17

The prevailing characteristics of the kingdom that Jesus represents are moral characteristics. There must be an alteration in me before I can be in the kingdom, or the kingdom can be in me, and that can be only by means of an inner crisis—regeneration. There must be something outside me which will alter me on the inside. GW 53

The majority of us know nothing whatever about the righteousness that is gifted to us in Jesus Christ. We are still trying to bring human nature up to a pitch it cannot reach, because there is something wrong with human nature. The old Puritanism which we are apt to ridicule did the same service for men that Pharisaism did for Saul, and that Roman Catholicism did for Luther; but nowadays we have no "iron" in us anywhere; we have no idea of righteousness; we do not care whether we are righteous or not. We have not only lost Jesus Christ's idea of righteousness, but we laugh at the Bible idea of righteousness; our god is the conventional righteousness of the society to which we belong. HG 12

∾ 114 ∾

THE GOD OF HOPE

READING: ROMANS 15

May the God of hope fill you with all joy and peace as you trust in him, so that you may overflow with hope by the power of the Holy Spirit.

ROMANS 15:13

Jesus Christ did not preach a gospel of hope: He came to reorganize humanity from the inside through a tremendous tragedy in His own life called the cross, and through that cross every member of the human race can be reinstated in God's favor and enter into a conscious inheritance of the atonement. BSG 64

The only hope for a man lies not in giving him an example of how to behave, but in the preaching of Jesus Christ as the Savior from sin. The heart of every man gets hope when he hears that. DI 64

∼115∼

BE WISE ABOUT WHAT IS GOOD

READING: ROMANS 16

Everyone has heard about your obedience, so I am full of joy over you; but I want you to be wise about what is good, and innocent about what is evil.

ROMANS 16:19

It has been a favorite belief in all ages that if only men were taught what good is, everyone would choose it; but history and human experience prove that that is not so. To know what good is is not to be good. DI 26

One might almost say that our every effort to be good and our every effort to be holy is a sure sign that we are neither good nor holy. A child makes no effort to be the daughter or son of its parents, and a child of God born of the Spirit makes no conscious effort to be good or to be holy; but just as a child trying to imitate someone else's mother is bound to fail, so the natural man trying to imitate God is bound to fail. GW 67

CORINTHIANS: WORKERS TOGETHER

～116～

THE CROSS, THE POWER OF GOD

READING: 1 CORINTHIANS 1–2

For the message of the cross is foolishness to those who are perishing, but to us who are being saved it is the power of God.

1 CORINTHIANS 1:18

The aspect of the cross in discipleship is lost altogether in the present-day view of following Jesus. The cross is looked upon as something beautiful and simple instead of a stern heroism. Our Lord never said it was easy to be a Christian; He warned men that they would have to face a variety of hardships, which He termed "bearing the cross." AUG 49

The Bible says that God Himself accepted the responsibility for sin; the cross is the proof that He did. It cost Jesus Christ to the last drop of blood to deal with "the vast evil of the world." CHI 45

～117～

FELLOW WORKERS

READING: 1 CORINTHIANS 3

For the wisdom of this world is foolishness in God's

137

sight. As it is written: "He catches the wise in their craftiness."

1 CORINTHIANS 3:19

The wisdom of today concerns itself chiefly with the origin of things and not with God; consequently, neither the philosopher nor the mystic has time for actual life. The wisdom of the Hebrews concerns itself with practical life, and recognizes that the basis of things is tragic. The Bible attitude to practical life is [foreign to] most of us because we are far away from the rooted and grounded confidence in God of the Hebrews. We do not think on Bible lines; we think on pagan lines, and only in our emotional life do we dabble in spirituality. Consequently, when we are hard hit, our religion finds us dumb; or if we do talk, we talk as pagans. SHH 58

∼118∼

BE FAITHFUL

READING: 1 CORINTHIANS 4–5

Now it is required that those who have been given a trust must prove faithful.

1 CORINTHIANS 4:2

Watch where Jesus went. The one dominant note in His life was to do His Father's will. His is not the way of wisdom or of success, but the way of faithfulness. LG 156

Being faithful to Jesus Christ is the most difficult thing we try to do today. We will be faithful to our work, to serving others, or to anything else, just don't ask us to be faithful to Jesus Christ. Many Christians become very impatient when we talk about faithfulness to Jesus. Our Lord is dethroned more deliberately by Christian workers than by the world. We treat God as if He were a machine designed only to bless us, and we think of Jesus as just another one of the workers.

The goal of faithfulness is not that we will do work for God, but that He will be free to do His work through us. God calls us to His service and places tremendous responsibilities on us. He expects no complaining on our part and offers no explanation on His part. God wants to use us as He used His own Son. MUH-UE 12/19

∼119∼

LAWSUITS AMONG BELIEVERS

READING: 1 CORINTHIANS 6

By his power God raised the Lord from the dead, and he will raise us also.

1 CORINTHIANS 6:14

Christ's resurrection deity means that He can take us into union with God, and the way into that relationship of oneness is by the cross and the resurrection. The weakest saint can experience the power of the deity of the Son of God if he is willing to "let go." The whole almighty power of God is on our behalf, and when we realize this, life becomes the implicit life of the child. No wonder Jesus said, "Let not your heart be troubled" (John 14:1)! The characteristic of the saintly life is abandon to God, not a settling down on our whiteness. God is not making hothouse plants, but sons and daughters of God, men and women with a strong family likeness to Jesus Christ. PR 115

∼120∼

PAUL ON MARRIAGE

READING: 1 CORINTHIANS 7
Those who marry will face many troubles in this life.
1 CORINTHIANS 7:28

The relationship of man and woman has been totally misrepresented. The revelation in the Bible is not that it is a question of the one being unequal to the other but of the two being one. "In the day that God created man, in the likeness of God made He him; male and female created He them and blessed them, and called their name Adam, in the day when they were created" (Gen. 5:1–2). SHH 106

God allows tribulation and anguish to come right to the threshold of our lives in order to prove to us that His life in us is more than a match for all that is against us. SHL 11

∼121∼

EATING FOOD SACRIFICED TO IDOLS

READING: 1 CORINTHIANS 8–9
There is but one God, the Father, from whom all things came and for whom we live; and there is but one Lord, Jesus Christ, through whom all things came and through whom we live.

1 CORINTHIANS 8:6

Jesus Christ is a fact; He is the most honorable and the holiest man, and two things necessarily follow: First, He is the least likely to be deceived about Himself; second, He is least likely to deceive anyone else. AUG 82

The task which confronted Jesus Christ was that He had to bring man, who is a sinner, back to God, forgive him his sin, and make him as holy as He is Himself; and He did it single-handedly. The revelation is that Jesus Christ, the last Adam, was "made to be sin for us," the thing which severed man from God, and that He put away sin by the sacrifice of Himself—"that we might become the righteousness of God in Him" (2 Cor. 5:21). He lifted the human race back, not to where it was in the first Adam, He lifted it back to where it never was—to where He is Himself. CHI 15

∼ 122 ∼

LESSONS FROM ISRAEL'S HISTORY

READING: 1 CORINTHIANS 10

No temptation has seized you except what is common to man. And God is faithful; he will not let you be tempted beyond what you can bear. But when you are tempted, he will also provide a way out so that you can stand up under it.

1 CORINTHIANS 10:13

We are apt to imagine that our Lord was only tempted once and that then His temptations were over. His temptations went on from the first moment of His conscious life to the last, because His holiness was not the holiness of Almighty God, but the holiness of man, which can only progress by means of the things that go against it. LG 152

Temptation must come, and we do not know what it is until we meet it. When we do meet it, we must not debate with God, but stand absolutely true to Him no matter what it costs us personally, and we will find that the onslaught will leave us with higher and purer affinities than before. PR 70

∼123∼

INSTRUCTIONS ON WORSHIP

READING: 1 CORINTHIANS 11

But if we judged ourselves, we would not come under judgment.

1 CORINTHIANS 11:31

Most of us suspend judgment about ourselves. We find reasons for not accusing ourselves entirely; consequently, when we find anything so definite and intense as the Bible revelation, we are apt to say it exaggerates, until we are smitten with the knowledge of what we are like in God's sight. OPG 54

Which of us would dare stand before God and say, "My God, judge me as I have judged my fellowmen"? We have judged our fellowmen as sinners; if God had judged us like that, we would be in hell. God judges us through the marvelous atonement of Jesus Christ. SSM 80

～124～

GIFTS OF THE SPIRIT

READING: 1 CORINTHIANS 12–13

And now these three remain: faith, hope and love. But the greatest of these is love.

1 CORINTHIANS 13:13

Love to be anything at all must be personal; to love without hating is an impossibility, and the stronger and more emphatic the love, the more intense is its obverse, hatred. God loves the world so much that He hates with a perfect hatred the thing that switched men wrong; and Calvary is the measure of His hatred. BE 32

God is love, not, God is loving. God and love are synonymous. Love is not an attribute of God; it is God; whatever God is, love is. If your conception of love does not agree with justice and judgment and purity and holiness, then your idea of love is wrong. It is not love you conceive of in your mind, but some vague infinite foolishness, all tears and softness and of infinite weakness. LG 9

～125～

EAGERLY DESIRE SPIRITUAL GIFTS

READING: 1 CORINTHIANS 14

Follow the way of love and eagerly desire spiritual gifts, especially the gift of prophecy.

1 CORINTHIANS 14:1

Love is difficult to define, but the working definition I would like to give is that "love is the sovereign preference of my person for another person, embracing everyone and everything in that preference." LG 21

The springs of love are in God, not in us. It is absurd to look for the love of God in our natural hearts; the love of God is only there when it has been shed abroad by the Holy Ghost. OBH 58

∼126∼

THE GOSPEL

READING: 1 CORINTHIANS 15
If only for this life we have hope in Christ, we are to be pitied more than all men. But Christ has indeed been raised from the dead, the firstfruits of those who have fallen asleep.

1 CORINTHIANS 15:19–20

The Bible points out that man's spirit is immortal, whether or not he is energized by the Spirit of God; that is, spirit never sleeps. Instead of the spirit sleeping at what we call death, at the breaking away of spirit from the body, the spirit is ten thousand-fold more awake. With the majority of us, our spirits are half-concealed while we are in this body. Remember, spirit and personality are synonymous, but as long as a man is in the body his personality is obscured. Immediately when he dies, his spirit is no more obscured; it is absolutely awake; no limitations now; man is face to face with everything else that is of spirit.

Soul and body depend on each other; spirit does not—spirit is immortal. Soul is simply the spirit expressing itself in the body. Immediately when the body goes, the soul is gone, but the moment the body is brought back, soul is brought back, and spirit, soul, and body will again be together. Spirit has never died, can never die, in the sense in which the body dies; the spirit is immortal, either in immortal life or in immortal death. There is no such thing as annihilation taught in the Bible. The separation of spirit from body and soul is temporary. The resurrection is the resurrection of the body. BP 259

∾127∾

BE ON YOUR GUARD

READING: 1 CORINTHIANS 16

Be on your guard; stand firm in the faith; be men of courage; be strong.

1 CORINTHIANS 16:13

There is a method of making disciples which is not sanctioned by our Lord. It is an excessive pressing of people to be reconciled to God in a way that is unworthy of the dignity of the gospel. The pleading is on the line of: Jesus has done so much for us; cannot we do something out of gratitude to Him? This method of getting people into relationship to God out of pity for Jesus is never recognized by our Lord. It does not put sin in its right place, nor does it put the more serious aspect of the gospel in its right place. Our Lord never pressed anyone to follow Him unconditionally; nor did He wish to be followed merely out of an impulse of enthusiasm. He

never pleaded, He never entrapped; He made discipleship intensely narrow and pointed out certain
things which could never be in those who followed
Him. Today there is a tendency to take the harsh-
ness out of our Lord's statements. What Jesus says
is hard; it is only easy when it comes to those who
are His disciples. AUG 49

∼128∼

GOD'S PROMISES ARE "YES" IN CHRIST

READING: 2 CORINTHIANS 1–2

For no matter how many promises God has made,
they are "Yes" in Christ. And so through him the
"Amen" is spoken by us to the glory of God.
2 CORINTHIANS 1:20

At times it appears as if God has not only forsaken
His Word, but has deliberately deceived us. We asked
Him for a particular thing, or related ourselves to Him
along a certain line, and expected that it would mean
the fullness of blessing, and actually it has meant the
opposite—upset, trouble, and difficulty all around,
and we are staggered, until we learn that by this very
discipline God is bringing us to the place of entire
abandonment to Himself.

Never settle down in the middle of the dance of
circumstances and say that you have been mistaken
in your natural interpretation of God's promise to
you because the immediate aftermath is devastation;
say that God did give you the promise, and stick to
it, and slowly God will bring you into the perfect,

detailed fulfillment of that promise. When and where the fulfillment will take place depends upon God and yourself, but never doubt the absolute fulfillment of God's Word, and remember that the beginning of the fulfillment lies in your acquiescence in God's will. Remain true to God, although it means the sword going through the natural, and you will be brought into a supernaturally clear agreement with God. We are not introduced to Christianity by explanations, but we must labor at the exposition of Christianity until we satisfactorily unfold it through God's grace and our own effort. NKW 22

～129～

THE SPIRIT AND FREEDOM

READING: 2 CORINTHIANS 3–4
Now the Lord is the Spirit, and where the Spirit of the Lord is, there is freedom.

2 CORINTHIANS 3:17

The reason man is not free is that within his personality there is a disposition which has been allowed to enslave his will, the disposition of sin. Man's destiny is determined by his disposition; he cannot alter his disposition, but he can choose to let God alter it. Jesus said, "Whosoever committeth sin is the servant of sin" (John 8:34); but He also said, "If the Son therefore shall make you free, ye shall be free indeed" (John 8:36), free in essence. We are free only when the Son sets us free, but we are free to choose whether or not we will be made free. MFL 28

~130~

ASSURANCE OF THE RESURRECTION

READING: 2 CORINTHIANS 5

Therefore, if anyone is in Christ, he is a new creation; the old has gone, the new has come!

2 CORINTHIANS 5:17

Jesus Christ claims that He can do in human nature what human nature cannot do for itself—"destroy the works of the devil" (1 John 3:8), remove the wrong heredity, and put in the right one. He can satisfy the last aching abyss of the human heart; He can put the key into our hands which will give the solution to every problem that ever stretched before our minds. He can soothe by His pierced hands the wildest sorrow with which Satan or sin or death ever racked humanity. There is nothing for which Jesus Christ is not amply sufficient and over which He cannot make us more than conquerors. BE 111

~131~

WORKERS TOGETHER

READING: 2 CORINTHIANS 6

As God's fellow workers we urge you not to receive God's grace in vain. For he says, "In the time of my favor I heard you, and in the day of salvation I helped you." I tell you, now is the time of God's favor, now is the day of salvation.

2 CORINTHIANS 6:1–2

The miracle of the grace of God is that He can make the past as though it had never been. RTR 33

Salvation is based on the revelation fact that God has redeemed the world from the possibility of condemnation on account of sin. The experience of salvation means that a man can be regenerated, can have the disposition of the Son of God put into him, meaning the Holy Spirit. DI 56

~132~

LET US PURIFY OURSELVES FROM EVIL

READING: 2 CORINTHIANS 7

Since we have these promises, dear friends, let us purify ourselves from everything that contaminates body and spirit, perfecting holiness out of reverence for God.

2 CORINTHIANS 7:1

Personal holiness is never the ground of my acceptance with God; the only ground of acceptance is the death of the Lord Jesus Christ. NKW 123

The one marvelous secret of a holy life is not in imitating Jesus, but in letting the perfections of Jesus manifest themselves in our mortal flesh. OBH 19

~133~

EXCEL IN GIVING

READING: 2 CORINTHIANS 8–9

But just as you excel in everything—in faith, in speech, in knowledge, in complete earnestness and in your love for us—see that you also excel in this grace of giving.

2 CORINTHIANS 8:7

If you feel remarkably generous, then be generous at once; act it out. If you don't, it will react and make you mean. BE 73

Our giving is to be proportionate to all we have received of the infinite giving of God. "Freely ye have received, freely give" (Matt. 10:8). Not how much we give, but what we do not give is the test of our Christianity. When we speak of giving, we nearly always think only of money. Money is the lifeblood of most of us. We have a remarkable trick—when we give money, we don't give sympathy; and when we give sympathy, we don't give money. CHI 77

∼134∼
OUR SPIRITUAL WARFARE

READING: 2 CORINTHIANS 10

The weapons we fight with are not the weapons of the world. On the contrary, they have divine power to demolish strongholds. We demolish arguments and every pretension that sets itself up against the knowledge of God, and we take captive every thought to make it obedient to Christ.

2 CORINTHIANS 10:4–5

Obedience is the basis of Christian thinking. Never be surprised if there are whole areas of thinking that are not clear; they never will be until you obey. DI 80

People won't go through the labor of thinking; consequently, snares get hold of them, and remember, thinking is a tremendous labor. We have to labor to "bring every thought into captivity to the obedience of Christ." GW 104

∼135∼

FALSE APOSTLES

READING: 2 CORINTHIANS 11

And no wonder, for Satan himself masquerades as an angel of light. It is not surprising, then, if his servants masquerade as servants of righteousness. Their end will be what their actions deserve.

2 CORINTHIANS 11:14–15

The pretensions of Satan are clear. He is the god of this world, and he will not allow relationship to the true God. Satan's attitude is that of a pretender to the throne; he claims it as his right. Wherever and whenever the rule of God is recognized by man, Satan proceeds to instill the tendency of mutiny and rebellion and lawlessness. BP 20

Satan . . . is as subtle as God is good, and he tries to counterfeit everything God does, and if he cannot counterfeit it, he will limit it. Do not be ignorant of his devices! BP 101

∼136∼

POWER MADE PERFECT IN WEAKNESS

READING: 2 CORINTHIANS 12

Three times I pleaded with the Lord to take it away from me. But he said to me, "My grace is sufficient

for you, for my power is made perfect in weakness."
Therefore I will boast all the more gladly about my
weaknesses, so that Christ's power may rest on me.

2 CORINTHIANS 12:8–9

"Be strong in the Lord" (Eph. 6:10). We much prefer to be strong *for* the Lord. The only way to be strong
in the Lord is to be "weak in Him." RTR 62

The source of physical strength in spiritual life is different from what it is in natural life. In natural life we
draw our strength direct from without, in spiritual life
we draw our physical strength, consciously or unconsciously, from communion with God. SHL 108

∼137∼

EXAMINE YOURSELVES

READING: 2 CORINTHIANS 13

Aim for perfection, listen to my appeal, be of one
mind, live in peace. And the God of love and peace
will be with you.

2 CORINTHIANS 13:11

We are to be perfect as our Father in heaven is perfect, not by struggle and effort, but by the impartation
of that which is perfect. IWP 9

God always ignores the present perfection for the
ultimate perfection. He is not concerned about making you blessed and happy just now; He is working
out His ultimate perfection all the time "that they may
be one even as We are" (John 17:11). MUH 118

Galatians to Thessalonians: Essentials of the Christian Life

∼138∼

Only One Gospel

READING: GALATIANS 1

The Lord Jesus Christ . . . gave himself for our sins to rescue us from the present evil age, according to the will of our God and Father.

GALATIANS 1:3–4

The salvation of God does not stand on human logic; it stands on the sacrificial death of Jesus. We can be born again because of the atonement of our Lord. Sinful men and women can be changed into new creatures, not by their repentance or their belief, but by the marvelous work of God in Christ Jesus, which is prior to all experience. The impregnable safety of justification and sanctification is God Himself. We have not to work out these things ourselves; they have been worked out by the atonement. The supernatural becomes natural by the miracle of God; there is the realization of what Jesus Christ has already done—"It is finished." MUH 302

∼139∼

DEFENDING THE GOSPEL

READING: GALATIANS 2

I have been crucified with Christ and I no longer live, but Christ lives in me. The life I live in the body, I live by faith in the Son of God, who loved me and gave himself for me.

GALATIANS 2:20

The teaching of self-realization is the great opponent of the doctrine of sanctification. "I have to realize myself as a separate individual, must educate and develop myself so that I fulfill the purpose of my being." Self-realization and self-consciousness are ways in which the principle of sin works out, and in Galatians 2:20 Paul is referring to the time and the place where he got rid of his "soul" in this respect. There is nothing in the nature of self-realization or of self-consciousness in our Lord.

People will say glibly, "Oh yes, I have been crucified with Christ," while their whole life is stamped with self-realization. Once identification with the death of Jesus has really taken place, self-realization does not appear again. To be "crucified with Christ" means that in obedience to the Spirit granted to me at regeneration, I eagerly and willingly go to the cross and crucify self-realization forever. The crucifixion of the flesh is the willing action of an obedient regenerate man or woman. "And they that are Christ's have crucified the flesh with the affections and lusts" (Gal. 5:24). Obey the Spirit of God and the Word of God, and it will be as clear as a sunbeam what you have to do; it is an attitude of will toward

God, an absolute abandon, a glad sacrifice of the soul in unconditional surrender. Then comes the marvelous revelation: "I have been crucified with Christ," not, "I am being crucified," or, "I hope to be crucified by and by"; not, "I am getting nearer to the place where I shall be crucified with Christ," but, "I have been crucified with Christ—I realize it and know it." BE 89

∼ 140 ∼

FAITH OR THE LAW?

READING: GALATIANS 3

Clearly no one is justified before God by the law, because, "The righteous will live by faith."

GALATIANS 3:11

We all have faith in good principles, in good management, in good common sense, but who among us has faith in Jesus Christ? Physical courage is grand, moral courage is grander, but the man who trusts Jesus Christ in the face of the terrific problems of life is worth a whole crowd of heroes. HG 61

The reason people disbelieve God is not because they do not understand with their heads—we understand very few things with our heads—but because they have turned their hearts in another direction. BP 144

∼ 141 ∼

NO LONGER A SLAVE, BUT A SON

READING: GALATIANS 4

So you are no longer a slave, but a son; and since you

are a son, God has made you also an heir.

GALATIANS 4:7

Why does God take such a long time? Because of what He is after—"bringing many sons unto glory" (Heb. 2:10). It takes time to make a son. We are not made sons of God by magic; we are saved in the great supernatural sense by the sovereign work of God's grace, but sonship is a different matter. I have to become a son of God by deliberate discernment and understanding and chastisement, not by spiritual necromancy, imagining I can ascend to heaven in leaps and bounds. The "shortcut" would make men mechanisms, not sons, with no discernment of God. If God did not shield His only begotten Son from any of the requirements of sonship (see Heb. 5:8), He will not shield us from all the requirements of being His sons and daughters by adoption. PH 100

∼ 142 ∼

STAND FIRM AND LIVE BY THE SPIRIT

READING: GALATIANS 5

So I say, live by the Spirit, and you will not gratify the desires of the sinful nature.

GALATIANS 5:16

The Holy Ghost is seeking to awaken men out of lethargy. He is pleading, yearning, blessing, pouring benedictions on men, convicting and drawing them nearer, for one purpose only, that they may receive Him so that He may make them holy men and women exhibiting the life of Jesus Christ. BE 99

∼143∼

WE REAP WHAT WE SOW

READING: GALATIANS 6

The one who sows to please his sinful nature, from that nature will reap destruction; the one who sows to please the Spirit, from the Spirit will reap eternal life.

GALATIANS 6:8

Carnality undisguised is hell. It is adulterous, fornicating, unclean, lascivious, idolatrous, spiritualistic, hateful, at variance, emulating, wrathful, a strife maker, seditious, a heretic, envious, murderous, a drunkard, a reveller, and so on (Gal. 5:19–20). Carnality shall have its part in the lake which burns with fire and brimstone (Rev. 21:8).

Sanctification discerns whatsoever things are true, whatsoever things are just, whatsoever things are pure, whatsoever things are lovely, whatsoever things are of good report. Sanctification discerns any virtue and anything praiseworthy and delights in these. Sanctification and spiritual discernment are easily entreated, full of mercy and good fruits, and never seem what they are not (see James 3:17). GR 1/31/1907

∼144∼

EVERY SPIRITUAL BLESSING FROM CHRIST

READING: EPHESIANS 1

Praise be to the God and Father of our Lord Jesus Christ, who has blessed us in the heavenly realms with every spiritual blessing in Christ.

EPHESIANS 1:3

Any man, every man, we ourselves, may partake of this marvelous raising up whereby God puts us into the wonderful life of His Son, and the very qualities of Jesus Christ are imparted to us. There is plenty of room to grow in the heavenly places; room for the head to grow, for the heart to grow, for the bodily relationships to grow, for the spirit to grow—plenty of room for every phase of us to grow into the realization of what a marvelous being our Lord Jesus Christ is. OBH 32

"Heavenly places in Christ Jesus." That is where God raises us. We do not get there by climbing, by aspiring, by struggling, by consecration, or by vows; God lifts us right straight up out of sin, inability and weakness, lust and disobedience, wrath and self-seeking—lifts us right up out of all this, "up, up to the whiter than snow shine," to the heavenly places where Jesus Christ lived when He was on earth, and where He lives to this hour in the fullness of the plenitude of His power. May God never relieve us from the wonder of it. We are lifted up into that inviolable place that cannot be defiled, and Paul states that God can raise us up there *now,* and that the wonder of sitting in the heavenly places in Christ Jesus is to be manifested in our lives while we are here on earth. OBH 32

∼145∼

GOD'S WORKMANSHIP, ALIVE IN CHRIST

READING: EPHESIANS 2

We are God's workmanship, created in Christ Jesus to do good works, which God prepared in advance for us to do.

EPHESIANS 2:10

To recognize that my Lord counts us faithful removes the last snare of idealizing natural pluck. If we have the idea that we must face the difficulties with pluck, we have never recognized the truth that He has counted us faithful; it is His work in me He is counting worthy, not my work for Him. The truth is we have nothing to fear and nothing to overcome because He is all in all, and we are more than conquerors through Him. The recognition of this truth is not flattering to the worker's sense of heroics, but it is amazingly glorifying to the work of Christ. He counts us worthy because He has done everything for us. It is a shameful thing for Christians to talk about "getting the victory"; by this time the Victor ought to have got us so completely that it is His victory all the time, not ours. AUG 11

∼146∼

GOD'S SECRET PLAN

READING: EPHESIANS 3

In [Christ] and through faith in him we may approach God with freedom and confidence.

EPHESIANS 3.12

So many of us limit our praying because we are not reckless in our confidence in God. In the eyes of those who do not know God, it is madness to trust Him, but when we pray in the Holy Ghost we begin to realize the resources of God, that He is our perfect heavenly Father, and we are His children. IYA 62

A great point is reached spiritually when we stop worrying God over personal matters or over any matter. God expects of us the one thing that glorifies Him—and that is to remain absolutely confident in Him, remembering what He has said beforehand, and sure that His purpose will be fulfilled. RTR 67

~147~

WALK IN UNITY

READING: EPHESIANS 4

[Christ] gave [gifts] . . . to prepare God's people for works of service, so that the body of Christ may be built up until we all reach unity in the faith . . . and become mature.

EPHESIANS 4:11–13

If we are paying attention to the source, rivers of living water will pour out of us, but if immediately we stop paying attention to the source, the outflow begins to dry up. We have nothing to do with our "useability," but only with our relationship to Jesus Christ; nothing must be allowed to come in between. IWP 45

Whether our work is a success or a failure has nothing to do with us. Our call is not to successful service, but to faithfulness. SSY 123

~148~

LIVE AS CHILDREN OF LIGHT

READING: EPHESIANS 5

For you were once darkness, but now you are light in the Lord. Live as children of light.

EPHESIANS 5:8

Nothing is cleaner or grander or sweeter than light. Light cannot be soiled; a sunbeam may shine into the dirtiest puddle, but it is never soiled. A sheet of white paper can be soiled, as can almost any white substance, but you cannot soil light. BP 173

"Let your light so shine before men" (Matt. 5:16). Our light is to shine in the darkness; it is not needed in the light. OBH 75

∼149∼

PUT ON THE FULL ARMOR OF GOD

READING: EPHESIANS 6

Put on the full armor of God so that you can take your stand against the devil's schemes.

EPHESIANS 6:11

"Wherefore take unto you the whole armor of God." It is not given; we have to take it. It is there for us to put on, understanding what we are doing. We have the idea that prayer is for special times, but we have to put on the armor of God for the continual practice of prayer, so that any struggling onslaught of the powers of darkness cannot touch the position of prayer. When we pray easily, it is because Satan is completely defeated in his onslaughts; when we pray difficultly, it is because Satan is gaining a victory. We have not been continuously practicing; we have not been facing things courageously; we have not been taking our orders from our Lord. Our Lord did not say, "Go" or, "Do"; He said, "Watch and pray."

If we struggle in prayer, it is because the enemy is gaining ground. If prayer is simple to us, it is because we have the victory. There is no such thing as a holiday for the beating of your heart. If there is, the grave comes next. And there is no such thing as a moral or spiritual holiday. If we attempt to take a holiday, the next time we want to pray it is a struggle because the enemy has gained a victory all round, darkness has come down, and spiritual wickedness in high places has enfolded us. If we have to fight, it is because we have disobeyed; we ought to be more than conquerors. IYA 33

∼150∼

LIVE WORTHY OF THE GOSPEL

READING: PHILIPPIANS 1

Whatever happens, conduct yourselves in a manner worthy of the gospel of Christ.

PHILIPPIANS 1:27

Righteousness means living and acting in accordance with right and justice, that is, it must express itself in a man's bodily life. "Little children, let no man deceive you: he that doeth righteousness is righteous" (1 John 3:7). CHI 81

It is righteous behavior that brings blessing on others, and the heart of faith sees that God is working things out well. HG 45

∼151∼

BE HUMBLE

READING: PHILIPPIANS 2

Do nothing out of selfish ambition or vain conceit, but

in humility consider others better than yourselves.
PHILIPPIANS 2:3

If my love is first of all for God, I shall take no account of the base ingratitude of others, because the mainspring of my service to my fellowmen is love to God. BP 181

The evidence that we are in love with God is that we identify ourselves with His interest in others, and other people are the exact expression of what we ourselves are; that is the humiliating thing! PR 107

～ 152 ～

DO NOT BE ANXIOUS

READING: PHILIPPIANS 3–4

Do not be anxious about anything, but in everything, by prayer and petition, with thanksgiving, present your requests to God.

PHILIPPIANS 4:6

"Take no thought for your life" (Matt. 6:25). These words of our Lord are the most revolutionary of statements. We argue in exactly the opposite way, even the most spiritual of us—"I *must* live, I *must* make so much money, I *must* be clothed and fed." That is how it begins; the great concern of the life is not God, but how we are going to fit ourselves to live. Jesus Christ says, "Reverse the order, get rightly related to Me first, see that you maintain that as the great care of your life, and never put the concentration of your care on the other things." SSM 68

163

It is useless to mistake careful consideration of circumstances for that which produces character. We cannot produce an inner life by watching the outer all the time. The lily obeys the law of its life in the surroundings in which it is placed, and Jesus says, as a disciple, consider your hidden life with God; pay attention to the source and God will look after the outflow. Imagine a lily hauling itself out of its pot and saying, "I don't think I look exactly right here." The lily's duty is to obey the law of its life where it is placed by the gardener. "Watch your life with God," says Jesus. "See that that is right and you will grow as the lily." We are all inclined to say, "I should be all right if only I were somewhere else." There is only one way to develop spiritually, and that is by concentrating on God. Don't bother about whether you are growing in grace or whether you are being of use to others, but believe on Jesus and out of you will flow rivers of living water. SSM 69

～153～

SUPREMACY OF CHRIST

READING: COLOSSIANS 1

He is the image of the invisible God, the firstborn over all creation. For by him all things were created: things in heaven and on earth, visible and invisible, whether thrones or powers or rulers or authorities; all things were created by him and for him.

COLOSSIANS 1:15–16

Jesus Christ is God manifest in the flesh, not a being with two personalities. He is Son of God (the exact expression of Almighty God) and Son of Man (the presentation of God's normal man). As Son of God, He reveals what God is like; as Son of Man, He mirrors what the human race will be like on the basis of redemption—a perfect oneness between God and man. SA 35

The character of Jesus Christ is exhibited in the New Testament and it appeals to us all. He lived His life straight down in the ordinary amalgam of human life, and He claims that the character He manifested is possible for any man if he will come in by the door He provides. AUG 81

∼154∼

ALIVE WITH CHRIST

READING: COLOSSIANS 2

When you were dead in your sins . . . , God made you alive with Christ. He forgave us all our sins, having canceled the written code, with its regulations, that was against us and that stood opposed to us; he took it away, nailing it to the cross.

COLOSSIANS 2:13–14

Either the cross is the only way there is of explaining God, the only way of explaining Jesus Christ, and of explaining the human race, or there is nothing in it at all. BE 61

The cross did not happen to Jesus: He came on purpose for it. BSG 40

The cross of Christ alone makes me holy, and it does so the second I am willing to let it. GW 54

∼155∼
SET YOUR HEARTS ON THINGS ABOVE

READING: COLOSSIANS 3

Since, then, you have been raised with Christ, set your hearts on things above, where Christ is seated at the right hand of God.

COLOSSIANS 3:1

The heart is the altar of which the physical body is the outer court, and whatever is offered on the altar of the heart will tell ultimately through the extremities of the body. "Keep thy heart with all diligence, for out of it are the issues of life" (Prov. 4:23). MFL 113

The human heart must have satisfaction, but there is only one being who can satisfy the last aching abyss of the human heart, and that is our Lord Jesus Christ. PH 52

∼156∼
DEVOTE YOURSELVES TO PRAYER

READING: COLOSSIANS 4

Devote yourselves to prayer, being watchful and thankful.

COLOSSIANS 4:2

If we look only for results in the earthlies when we pray, we are ill-taught. A praying saint performs far more havoc among the unseen forces of darkness than we have the slightest notion of. "The effectual fervent prayer of a righteous man availeth much" (James 5:16). BP 159

There is only one field of service that has no snares, and that is the field of intercession. All other fields have the glorious but risky snare of publicity; prayer has not. IYA 96

∼157∼

EXAMPLES OF TRUE BELIEVERS

READING: 1 THESSALONIANS 1–2

When you received the word of God . . . , you accepted it not as the word of men, but as it actually is, the word of God, which is at work in you who believe.

1 THESSALONIANS 2:13

To use the New Testament as a book of proof is nonsense. If you do not believe that Jesus Christ is the Son of God, the New Testament will not convince you that He is; if you do not believe in the resurrection, the New Testament will not convince you of it. The New Testament is written for those who do not need convincing. HGM 35

A remarkable thing about this book of God is that for every type of human being we come across there is a distinct, clear line laid down here as to the way to apply God's truth to it. The stupid soul, the stubborn soul, the soul that is mentally diseased, the soul that is convicted of sin, the soul with the twisted mind, the sensual soul—every one of the facts that you meet in your daily walk and business has its counterpart here, and God has a word and a revelation fact with regard to every life you come across. WG 13

∼158∼

BE BLAMELESS AND HOLY

READING: 1 THESSALONIANS 3

May [the Lord] strengthen your hearts so that you will be blameless and holy in the presence of our God and Father when our Lord Jesus comes with all his holy ones.

1 THESSALONIANS 3:13

If we are sanctified by the power of the God of peace, our self life is blameless before Him. There is nothing to hide, and the more we bring our soul under the searchlight of God, the more we realize the ineffable comfort of the supernatural work He has done. LG 139

Can God keep me from stumbling this second? Yes. Can He keep me from sin this second? Yes. Well, that is the whole of life; you cannot live more than a second at a time. If God can keep you blameless this second, He can do it the next. No wonder Jesus Christ said, "Let not your heart be troubled" (John 14:1). We do get troubled when we do not remember the amazing power of God. LG 144

∼159∼

A CALL TO A HOLY LIFE

READING: 1 THESSALONIANS 4

For God did not call us to be impure, but to live a holy life.

1 THESSALONIANS 4:7

The purity God demands is impossible unless we can be remade from within, and that is what Jesus Christ undertakes to do through the atonement. BE 10

He will keep your heart so pure that you would tremble with amazement if you knew how pure the atonement of the Lord Jesus can make the vilest human heart, if we will but keep in the light, as God is in the light. BP 124

～160～

BE READY, BE JOYFUL

READING: 1 THESSALONIANS 5

Be joyful always; pray continually; give thanks in all circumstances, for this is God's will for you in Christ Jesus.

1 THESSALONIANS 5:16–18

We are not responsible for the circumstances we are in, but we are responsible for the way we allow those circumstances to affect us; we can either allow them to get on top of us, or we can allow them to transform us into what God wants us to be. CHI 40

When we know that nothing can separate us from the love of Christ, it does not matter what calamities may occur; we are as unshakable as God's throne. CD VOL. 1 157

～161～

GOD WILL SET MATTERS RIGHT

READING: 2 THESSALONIANS 1–2:12

Your faith is growing more and more . . . [and] we boast about your perseverance and faith in all the persecutions and trials you are enduring.

2 THESSALONIANS 1:3–4

Jesus Christ not only warned that persecution would come, He went further and said that it was profitable to go through persecution. "Blessed are ye, when men shall . . . persecute you" (Matt. 5:11). The way the world treats me is the exhibition of my inner disposition. "Whosoever maketh himself a friend of the world is the enemy of God" (James 4:4). SHL 16

To have brickbats and rotten eggs flung at you is not persecution; it simply makes you feel good and does you no harm at all. But when your own crowd cuts you dead and systematically vexes you, then says Jesus, "Count it all joy." "Blessed are ye when men shall hate you, and when they shall separate you from their company, and shall reproach you, and cast out your name as evil, for the Son of man's sake" (Luke 6:22), not for the sake of some crotchety notion of our own. SHL 16

∼ 162 ∼

STAND FIRM AND DO WHAT IS RIGHT

READING: 2 THESSALONIANS 2:13–3
And as for you, brothers, never tire of doing what is right.

2 THESSALONIANS 3:13

God's "ought's" never alter; we never grow out of them. Our difficulty is that we find in ourselves this attitude: "I ought to do this, but I won't"; "I ought to do that, but I don't want to." That puts out of court the idea that if you teach men what is right, they will do it. They won't; what is needed is a power which will enable a man to do what he knows is right. BE 8

"Except your righteousness shall exceed the righteousness of the scribes and Pharisees" (Matt. 5:20)—not be different from but "exceed," that is, we have to be all they are and infinitely more! We have to be right in our external behavior, but we have to be as right and "righter" in our internal behavior. We have to be right in our words and actions, but we have to be right in our thoughts and feelings. RTR 59

Timothy to Hebrews: Running the Race

～163～

Beware of False Teachers

Reading: 1 Timothy 1–2

Christ Jesus came into the world to save sinners—of whom I am the worst.

1 Timothy 1:15

God made His own Son to be sin that He might make the sinner a saint. The Bible reveals all through that Jesus Christ bore the sin of the world by identification, not by sympathy. He deliberately took upon Himself and bore in His own person the whole massed sin of the human race, and by so doing He rehabilitated the human race, that is, put it back to where God designed it to be, and anyone can enter into union with God on the ground of what our Lord did on the cross. AUG 71

The New Testament says Jesus became literally identified with the sin of the human race. Him who knew no sin (here language almost fails) He made Him to be sin for us for one purpose only—"that we might become the righteousness of God in Him" (2 Cor. 5:21). BSG 26

∼164∼

Set an Example

READING: 1 Timothy 3–4

Set an example for the believers in speech, in life, in love, in faith and in purity.

1 Timothy 4:12

The problems of life get hold of a man and make it difficult for him to know whether in the face of these things he really is confident in Jesus Christ. The attitude of a believer must be, "Things do look black, but I believe Him; and when the whole thing is told I am confident my belief will be justified and God will be revealed as a God of love and justice." It does not mean that we won't have problems, but it does mean that our problems will never come in between us and our faith in Him. AUG 114

Believe what you do believe and stick to it, but don't profess to believe more than you intend to stick to. If you say you believe God is love, stick to it, [despite] a pandemonium shouting that God is cruel to allow what He does. DI 12

A believer is one whose whole being is based on the finished work of redemption. DI 1

∼165∼

Advice about Widows and Elders

READING: 1 Timothy 5

The elders who direct the affairs of the church well

are worthy of double honor, especially those whose work is preaching and teaching.

1 TIMOTHY 5:17

Don't preach salvation; don't preach holiness; don't preach the baptism of the Holy Ghost; preach Jesus Christ and everything else will take its right place. GW 48

If you are a teacher sent from God, your worth in God's sight is estimated by the way you enable people to see Jesus. IWP 112

～166～

THE ROOT OF EVIL

READING: 1 TIMOTHY 6

The love of money is a root of all kinds of evil. Some people, eager for money, have wandered from the faith and pierced themselves with many griefs.

1 TIMOTHY 6:10

The two things around which our Lord centered His most scathing teaching were money and marriage, because they are the two things that make men and women devils or saints. Covetousness is the root of all evil, whether it shows itself in money matters or in any way. HG 23

If we listen to what our Lord says about money, we shall see how we disbelieve Him. We quietly ignore all He says; He is so unpractical, so utterly stupid from the modern standpoint. MFL 125

～167～

GUARD YOUR FAITH

READING: 2 TIMOTHY 1

I am not ashamed, because I know whom I have believed, and am convinced that he is able to guard what I have entrusted to him for that day.

2 TIMOTHY 1:12

The one thing that tells is the great fundamental rock: "Believe also in Me" (John 14:1). Many know a good deal about salvation, but not much about this intense patience of "hanging in" in perfect certainty to the fact that what Jesus Christ says is true. AUG 117

Belief is a wholesome committal; it means making things inevitable, cutting off every possible retreat. Belief is as irrevocable as bereavement. DI 1

～168～

BE STRONG AND ENDURE HARDSHIP

READING: 2 TIMOTHY 2

You then, my son, be strong in the grace that is in Christ Jesus. . . . Endure hardship with us like a good soldier of Christ Jesus.

2 TIMOTHY 2:1, 3

No power on earth or in hell can conquer the Spirit of God in human spirit; it is an inner unconquerableness. If you have the whine in you, kick it out ruthlessly. It is a positive crime to be weak in God's strength. RTR 65

The realization that my Lord has enabled me to be a worker keeps me strong enough never to be weak. Conscious obtrusive weakness is natural unthankful strength; it means I refuse to be made strong by Him. When I say I am too weak, it means I am too strong; and whenever I say "I can't," it means "I won't." When Jesus Christ enables me, I am omnipotently strong all the time. AUG 11

∼169∼

PAUL'S CHARGE TO TIMOTHY

READING: 2 TIMOTHY 3–4
All Scripture is God-breathed and is useful for teaching, rebuking, correcting and training in righteousness.
2 TIMOTHY 3:16

The Bible is the only book that throws light on our physical condition, on our soul condition, and on our spiritual condition. In the Bible the sense of smell and sight and so on are not used as metaphors only; they are identified with the nature of the soul's life. This accounts for what people are apt to call the vulgar teaching of the Bible. BP 53

When a man's heart is right with God, the mysterious utterances of the Bible are "spirit and life" to him. BSG 42

∼170∼

LIVE GODLY BY GOD'S GRACE

READING: TITUS 1–2
For the grace of God that brings salvation . . . teaches us . . . to live self-controlled, upright and godly lives in this

present age, while we wait for the blessed hope—the glorious appearing of our great God and Savior, Jesus Christ.

TITUS 2:11–13

One of the greatest proofs that we are drawing on the grace of God is that we can be humiliated without the slightest trace of anything but the grace of God in us. Draw on the grace of God now, not presently. The one word in the spiritual vocabulary is *now*. AUG 128

If we know that we have received the unmerited favor of God and we do not give unmerited favor to other people, we are damned in that degree. HG 38

∼171∼

HEIRS WITH THE HOPE OF ETERNAL LIFE

READING: TITUS 3

Our Savior . . . saved us through the washing of rebirth and renewal by the Holy Spirit, whom he poured out on us generously through Jesus Christ our Savior, so that, having been justified by his grace, we might become heirs having the hope of eternal life.

TITUS 3:4–7

It is the "preaching of the cross" that produces the crisis we call new birth. We are in danger of preaching the new birth instead of proclaiming that which produces the new birth—the preaching of Jesus Christ, and Him crucified. GW 17

In new birth God does three impossible things, impossible, that is, from the rational standpoint. The first is to make a man's past as though it had never been; the second, to make a man all over again; and the third, to make a man as certain of God as God is of Himself. New birth does not mean merely salvation from hell, but something more radical, something which tells in a man's actual life. PH 183

∼172∼

NO LONGER A SLAVE BUT A DEAR BROTHER

READING: PHILEMON

I always thank my God as I remember you in my prayers, because I hear about your faith in the Lord Jesus and your love for all the saints.

PHILEMON 4–5

The life of faith is the life of a soul who has given over every other life but the life of faith. Faith is not an action of the mind, nor of the heart, nor of the will, nor of the sentiment; it is the centering of the entire man in God. CD VOL. 2 149

When we go through the trial of faith, we gain so much wealth in our heavenly banking account, and the more we go through the trial of faith the wealthier we become in the heavenly regions. OBH 103

∼173∼

THE SON, THE RADIANCE OF GOD'S GLORY

READING: HEBREWS 1–2

The Son is the radiance of God's glory and the exact representation of his being, sustaining all things by his powerful word.

HEBREWS 1:3

Jesus Christ had a two-fold personality: He was Son of God revealing what God is like, and Son of Man, revealing what man is to be like. BSG 77

Jesus Christ was not a being who became divine; He was the Godhead incarnated. PR 130

∼174∼

FIX YOUR THOUGHTS ON JESUS

READING: HEBREWS 3

Therefore, holy brothers, who share in the heavenly calling, fix your thoughts on Jesus, the apostle and high priest whom we confess.

HEBREWS 3:1

The great lack today is of people who will *think* along Christian lines; we know a great deal about salvation, but we do not go on to explore the "unsearchable riches of Christ" (Eph. 3:8). We do not know much about giving up the right to ourselves to Jesus Christ, or about the intense patience of "hanging in" in perfect certainty that what Jesus says is true. LG 133

The danger in spiritual matters is that we do not *think* godliness; we let ideas and conceptions of godliness lift us up at times, but we do not form the habit of godly thinking. Thinking godliness cannot be done in spurts; it is a steady habitual trend. MFL 93

∼175∼

GOD'S WORD—LIVING, ACTIVE, SHARP

READING: HEBREWS 4

For the word of God is living and active. Sharper than

any double-edged sword, it penetrates even to divid-
ing soul and spirit, joints and marrow; it judges the
thoughts and attitudes of the heart.

HEBREWS 4:12

Why should I believe a thing because it is in the
Bible? That is a perfectly legitimate question. There is
no reason why you should believe it; it is only when
the Spirit of God applies the Scriptures to the inward
consciousness that a man begins to understand their
living efficacy. If we try from the outside to fit the Bible
to an external standard, or to a theory of verbal inspi-
ration or any other theory, we are wrong. "Ye search
the Scriptures because ye think that in them ye have
eternal life; and these are they which bear witness of
Me; and ye will not come to Me, that ye may have life"
(John 5:39–40). BE 122

∽176∽

GOOD AND EVIL

READING: HEBREWS 5

You are slow to learn. . . . You need milk, not solid
food! . . . Solid food is for the mature, who by constant use have trained themselves to distinguish good
from evil.

HEBREWS 5:11–14

There are some things of which we must be ignorant, because knowledge of them comes in no other
way than by disobedience to God. In the life originally
designed for Adam, it was not intended that he should
be ignorant of evil, but that he should know evil

through understanding good. Instead, he ate of the fruit of the tree of knowledge of good and evil and thereby knew evil positively and good negatively; consequently, none of us knows the order God intended. The knowledge of evil that comes through the fall has given human nature a bias of insatiable curiosity about the bad, and only when we have been introduced into the kingdom of God do we know good and evil in the way God constituted man to know them. SHL 61–62

～177～

Let's Go On to Maturity

Reading: Hebrews 6

Therefore let us leave the elementary teachings about Christ and go on to maturity, not laying again the foundation of repentance from acts that lead to death, and of faith in God.

Hebrews 6:1

Spiritual maturity is not reached by the passing of the years, but by obedience to the will of God. BSG 15

God never destroys the work of His own hands, He removes what would pervert it, that is all. Maturity is the stage where the whole life has been brought under the control of God. CHI 85

～178～

Jesus, unlike Other High Priests

Reading: Hebrews 7

Unlike the other high priests, [Jesus] does not need to offer sacrifices day after day, first for his own sins, and then for the sins of the people. He sacrificed for their sins once for all when he offered himself.

HEBREWS 7:27

He deliberately laid down His life without any possibility of deliverance. There was no compulsion; it was a sacrifice made with a free mind. Nor was there anything of the impulsive about it; He laid down His life with a clear knowledge of what He was doing. Jesus understood what was coming; it was not a foreboding, but a certainty—not a catastrophe which might happen, but an ordained certainty in the decrees of God, and He knew it. GW 113

When we are identified with Jesus Christ, the Spirit of God would have us sacrifice ourselves for Him, point for point, as He did for His Father. We pray and wait, and need urging, and want the thrilling vision; but Jesus wants us to narrow and limit ourselves to one thing: clearly and intelligently knowing what we are doing. We deliberately lay down our lives for Him as He laid down His life for us in the purpose of God. GW 114

∼ 179 ∼

A NEW COVENANT

READING: HEBREWS 8

I will put my laws in their minds and write them on their hearts. I will be their God, and they will be my people.

HEBREWS 8:10

God's laws are not watered down to suit anyone; if God did that He would cease to be God. The moral law never alters for the noblest or the weakest; it remains abidingly and eternally the same. BE 8

Man has to fulfill God's laws in his physical life, in his mental and moral life, in his social and spiritual life, and to offend in one point is to be guilty of all. BE 15

∼ 180 ∼

The Perfect Sacrifice

Reading: Hebrews 9

Christ was sacrificed once to take away the sins of many people; and he will appear a second time, not to bear sin, but to bring salvation to those who are waiting for him.
Hebrews 9:28

The forgiveness of God penetrates to the very heart of His nature and to the very heart of man's nature. That is why God cannot forgive until a man realizes what sin is. DI 65

Think what God's forgiveness means: It means that He forgets away every sin. GW 11

We may talk as much as we like about forgiveness, but it will never make any difference to us unless we realize that we need it. HGM 101

∼ 181 ∼

Persevere to Gain the Promise

Reading: Hebrews 10

You need to persevere so that when you have done the will of God, you will receive what he has promised.
Hebrews 10:36

There is a distinct period in our experience when we cease to say, "Lord, show me Thy will," and the realization begins to dawn that we *are* God's will, and He can do with us what He likes. We wake up to the knowledge that we have the privilege of giving ourselves over to God's will. It is a question of being yielded to God. AUG 108

The will of God is the gladdest, brightest, most bountiful thing possible to conceive, and yet some of us talk of the will of God with a terrific sigh, "Oh well, I suppose it is the will of God," as if His will were the most calamitous thing that could befall us. IWP 19

How are we going to find out the will of God? "God will communicate it to us." He will not. His will is there all the time, but we have to discover it by being renewed in our minds, by taking heed to His Word and obeying it. MFL 80

∼182∼

BY FAITH WE UNDERSTAND

READING: HEBREWS 11

Now faith is being sure of what we hope for and certain of what we do not see.

HEBREWS 11:1

Certainty is the mark of the commonsense life; gracious uncertainty is the mark of the spiritual life. To be certain of God means that we are uncertain in all our ways; we do not know what a day may bring forth.

This is generally said with a sigh of sadness; it should be rather an expression of breathless expectation. We are uncertain of the next step, but we are certain of God. Immediately, we abandon to God, and do the duty that lies nearest; He packs our life with surprises all the time. MUH 120

When we become advocates of a creed, something dies; we do not believe God; we only believe our belief about Him. Jesus said, "Except ye . . . become as little children" (Matt. 18:3). Spiritual life is the life of a child. We are not uncertain of God but uncertain of what He is going to do next. If we are only certain in our beliefs, we get dignified and severe and have the ban of finality about our views; but when we are rightly related to God, life is full of spontaneous, joyful uncertainty and expectancy. MUH 120

～183～

God Disciplines Us for the Race

Reading: Hebrews 12

No discipline seems pleasant at the time, but painful. Later on, however, it produces a harvest of righteousness and peace for those who have been trained by it.

Hebrews 12:11

We can all see God in exceptional things, but it requires the culture of spiritual discipline to see God in every detail. MUH 319

God will not discipline us; we must discipline ourselves. God will not bring every thought and imagination into captivity; we have to do it. MUH 323

The element of discipline in the life of faith must never be lost sight of, because only by means of the discipline are we taught the difference between the natural interpretation of what we call good and what God means by "good." NKW 22

It may be that in our inner life Jesus is teaching us by the disciplining force of His delays. "I expected God to answer my prayer, but He has not." He is bringing us to the place where by obedience we shall see what it is He is after. PH 221

The resentment of discipline of any kind will warp the whole life away from God's purpose. RTR 11

There are many things that are perfectly legitimate, but if you are going to concentrate on God, you cannot do them. Your right hand is one of the best things you have, but Jesus says if it hinders you in following His precepts, cut it off. This line of discipline is the sternest one that ever struck mankind. RTR 91

∼184∼

OUR CHANGELESS SAVIOR

READING: HEBREWS 13

Jesus Christ is the same yesterday and today and forever.

HEBREWS 13:8

Jesus never asks anyone to define his position or to understand a creed, but, "Who am I to you?" . . . Jesus Christ makes the whole of human destiny depend on a man's relationship to Himself. AUG 82

The great life is to believe that Jesus Christ is not a fraud. AUG 114

The Jesus who saves our souls and identifies us with Himself is "this same Jesus" who went to sleep as a babe on His mother's bosom; and it is "this same Jesus," the almighty, powerful Christ, with all power in heaven and on earth, who is at work in the world today by His Spirit. BSG 72

Get into the habit of recalling to your mind what Jesus was like when He was here; picture what He did and what He said. Recall His gentleness and tenderness as well as His strength and sternness, and then say, "That is what God is like." CHI 77

Our Lord never worried, nor was He ever anxious, because He was not out to realize His own ideas. He was out to realize God's ideas. GW 81

Jesus Christ is not only Savior, He is King, and He has the right to exact anything and everything from us at His own discretion. HGM 129

Jesus Christ is the last word on God, on sin and death, on heaven and hell; the last word on every problem that human life has to face. IWP 125

Our Lord was not a recluse nor an ascetic; He did not cut Himself off from society, but He was inwardly disconnected all the time. He was not aloof, but He lived in another world. He was so much in the ordinary world that the religious people of His day called Him a glutton and wine-bibber. MUH 332

James to Jude: The Daily Walk

~185~

Consider Trials a Joy

Reading: James 1

Consider it pure joy, my brothers, whenever you face trials of many kinds, because you know that the testing of your faith develops perseverance.

James 1:2–3

We have no faith at all until it is proved, proved through conflict and in no other way. HGM 58

To walk with God means the perpetual realization of the nature of faith—that it must be tried or it is mere fancy; faith untried has no character value for the individual. OPG 18

There is nothing akin to faith in the natural world. Defiant pluck and courage is not faith; it is the *trial* of faith that is "much more precious than of gold," and the trial of faith is never without the essentials of temptation. OPG 18

~186~

Convicted by the Law

Reading: James 2

If you show favoritism, you sin and are convicted by the law as lawbreakers. For whoever keeps the whole law and yet stumbles at just one point is guilty of breaking all of it.

JAMES 2:9–10

The moral law does not consider our weaknesses as human beings; in fact, it does not take into account our heredity or infirmities. It simply demands that we be absolutely moral. The moral law never changes, either for the highest of society or for the weakest in the world. It is enduring and eternally the same. The moral law, ordained by God, does not make itself weak to the weak by excusing our shortcomings. It remains absolute for all time and eternity. If we are not aware of this, it is because we are less than alive. Once we do realize it, our life immediately becomes a fatal tragedy. "I was alive once without the law, but when the commandment came, sin revived and I died" (Rom. 7:9). The moment we realize this, the Spirit of God convicts us of sin. Until a person gets there and sees that there is no hope, the Cross of Christ remains absurd to him. Conviction of sin always brings a fearful, confining sense of the law. It makes a person hopeless—"sold under sin" (Rom. 7:14). I, a guilty sinner, can never work to get right with God. It is impossible. There is only one way by which I can get right with God, and that is through the death of Jesus Christ. I must get rid of the underlying idea that I can ever be right with God because of my obedience. Who of us could ever obey God to absolute perfection! MUH-UE 12/1

∼187∼

Tame the Tongue and Submit to God

Reading: James 3–4

Submit yourselves, then, to God. Resist the devil, and he will flee from you.

James 4:7

Relief in the redemption is difficult because it needs surrender first. I never can believe until I have surrendered myself to God. HG 106

Take an absolute plunge into the love of God, and when you are there you will be amazed at your foolishness for not getting there before. IWP 48

The tendency is strong to say, "Oh, God won't be so stern as to expect me to give up that!" *but He will;* "He won't expect me to walk in the light so that I have nothing to hide," *but He will;* "He won't expect me to draw on His grace for everything," *but He will.* RTR 3

∼188∼

Pray for Each Other

Reading: James 5

Therefore confess your sins to each other and pray for each other so that you may be healed. The prayer of a righteous man is powerful and effective.

James 5:16

The prayers of some people are more efficacious than those of others, the reason being that they are under no delusion. They do not rely on their own earnestness; they rely absolutely on the supreme authority of the Lord Jesus Christ. PR 126

Intercessory prayer is part of the sovereign purpose of God. If there were no saints praying for us, our lives would be infinitely balder than they are; consequently, the responsibility of those who never intercede and who are withholding blessing from other lives is truly appalling. CD VOL. 2 57

∼189∼

BE HOLY

READING: 1 PETER 1

But just as he who called you is holy, so be holy in all you do; for it is written: "Be holy, because I am holy."
1 PETER 1:15–16

Wherever Jesus comes, He reveals that man is away from God by reason of sin, and man is terrified at His presence. That is why men will put anything in the place of Jesus Christ, anything rather than let God come near in His startling purity, because immediately when God comes near, conscience records that God is holy and nothing unholy can live with Him; consequently, His presence hurts the sinner. "If I had not come and spoken unto them, they had not had sin: but now they have no cloak for their sin" (John 15:22). PS 62

You can never make yourself holy by external acts, but if you are holy, your external acts will be the natural expression of holiness. RTR 23

∼190∼

A CHOSEN PEOPLE

READING: 1 PETER 2

But you are a chosen people, a royal priesthood, a holy nation, a people belonging to God, that you may declare the praises of him who called you out of darkness into his wonderful light.

1 PETER 2:9

There is no variableness in God, no "shadow that is cast by turning." We are told that where there is light and substance, there must be shadow; but there is no shadow in God, none whatever. BP 219

In actual life we must be always in the light, and we cease to be in the light when we want to explain why we did a thing. The significant thing about our Lord is that He never explained anything; He let mistakes correct themselves because He always lived in the light. There is so much in us that is folded and twisted, but the sign that we are following God is that we keep in the light. LG 66

To walk in the light means that everything that is of the darkness drives me closer into the center of the light. MUH 361

∼191∼

CHRIST DIED TO BRING YOU TO GOD

READING: 1 PETER 3

For Christ died for sins once for all, the righteous for the unrighteous, to bring you to God.

1 PETER 3:18

Many people are never guilty of gross sins. They are not brought up in that way. They are too refined, have too much good taste, but that does not mean that the disposition to sin is not there. The essence of sin is my claim to my right to myself. I may prefer to live morally because it is better for me. I am responsible to no one; my conscience is my god. That is the very essence of sin. MFL 22

To be born of God means that I have the supernatural power of God to stop sinning. In the Bible it is never, Should a Christian sin? The Bible puts it emphatically: *A Christian must not sin.* The effective working of the new birth life in us is that we do not commit sin, not merely that we have the power not to sin, but that we have stopped sinning. MUH 228

～192～
REJOICE IF YOU SUFFER AS A CHRISTIAN

READING: 1 PETER 4–5
If you suffer as a Christian, do not be ashamed, but praise God that you bear that name.

1 PETER 4:16

Why there should be suffering we do not know; but we have to remain loyal to the character of God as revealed by Jesus Christ in the face of it. BE 93

The saint knows not why he suffers as he does, yet he comprehends with a knowledge that passeth knowledge that all is well. CD VOL. 2 105

To choose to suffer means that there is something wrong; to choose God's will even if it means suffering

194

is a very different thing. No healthy saint ever chooses suffering; He chooses God's will, as Jesus did, whether it means suffering or not. MUH 223

∾ 193 ∾

DIVINE POWER FOR THE BELIEVER

READING: 2 PETER 1

His divine power has given us everything we need for life and godliness through our knowledge of him who called us by his own glory and goodness.

2 PETER 1:3

The one who made the world and who upholds all things by the word of His power is the one who keeps His saints. GW 44

Before we were saved we had not the power to obey, but now that He has planted in us on the ground of redemption the heredity of the Son of God, we have the power to obey, and, consequently, the power to disobey. SSM 104

∾ 194 ∾

BEWARE OF FALSE TEACHERS

READING: 2 PETER 2

There were also false prophets among the people, just as there will be false teachers among you. They will secretly introduce destructive heresies, even denying the sovereign Lord who bought them—bringing swift destruction on themselves.

2 PETER 2:1

Jesus Christ is not a great teacher alongside Plato and other great teachers; He stands absolutely alone.

"Test your teachers," said Jesus; the teachers who come from God are those who clear the way to Jesus Christ, and keep it clear. We are estimated in God's sight as workers by whether or not we clear the way for people to see Jesus. HGM 125

If once you get the thought, "It is my winsome way of putting it, my presentation of the truth that attracts," the only name for that is the ugly name of thief, stealing the hearts of the sheep of God who do not know why they stop at you. Keep the mind stayed on God, and I defy anyone's heart to stop at you; it will always go on to God. IWP 112

∼195∼

GOD WILL KEEP HIS PROMISE

READING: 2 PETER 3

The Lord is not slow in keeping his promise, as some understand slowness. He is patient with you, not wanting anyone to perish, but everyone to come to repentance.

2 PETER 3:9

Jesus says we are to keep the word of His patience. There are so many things in this life that it seems much better to be impatient about. The best illustration is that of an archer. He pulls the string farther and farther away from his bow with the arrow fixed; then, when it is adjusted, with his eye on the mark, he lets fly. The Christian's life is like that. God is the archer: He takes the saint like a bow which he stretches, and we get to a certain point and say, "I can't stand any more; I can't stand this test of patience any longer," but God goes on stretching. He is not aiming at our mark, but at His own, and the patience of the saints is that we hold on until He lets the arrow fly straight to His goal. PH 149

∼196∼

WALK IN THE LIGHT

READING: 1 JOHN 1
If we walk in the light, as he is in the light, we have fellowship with one another, and the blood of Jesus, his Son, purifies us from all sin.

1 JOHN 1:7

"If we walk in the light as He is in the light . . . the blood of Jesus Christ His Son cleanseth us from all sin." That is cleansing not from conscious sin only but from infinitely more; it is cleansing to the depths of crystalline purity so that God Himself can see nothing impure. That is the work of the Lord Jesus Christ; to make His work anything less would be blasphemous. LG 142

He will keep your heart so pure that you would tremble with amazement if you knew how pure the atonement of the Lord Jesus can make the vilest human heart, if we will but keep in the light, as God is in the light. BP 124

∼197∼

WALKING IN OBEDIENCE

READING: 1 JOHN 2
We know that we have come to know him if we obey his commands.

1 JOHN 2:3

It is not a question of being willing to go straight through, but of going straight through. Not a question of saying, "Lord, I will do it," but of doing it. There must be the reckless committal of everything to Him with no regard for the consequences. GW 79

God never insists on our obedience; human authority does. Our Lord does not give us rules and regulations; He makes very clear what the standard is, and if the relation of my spirit to Him is that of love, I will do all He wants me to do without the slightest hesitation. If I begin to object, it is because I love someone else in competition with Him—myself. HGM 148

Jesus Christ's first obedience was to the will of His Father, and our first obedience is to be to Him. The thing that detects where we live spiritually is the word obey. The natural heart of man hates the word, and that hatred is the essence of the disposition that will not let Jesus Christ rule. MFL 114

∼198∼

WE ARE GOD'S CHILDREN

READING: 1 JOHN 3

Now we are children of God, and what we will be has not yet been made known. But we know that when he appears, we shall be like him, for we shall see him as he is.

1 JOHN 3:2

When we are rightly related to God as Jesus was, the spiritual life becomes as natural as the life of a child. BSG 14

Jesus Christ uses the child-spirit as a touchstone for the character of a disciple. He did not put up a child before His disciples as an ideal, but as an expression of the simple-hearted life they would live when they were born again. The life of a little child is expectant, full of wonder, and free from self-consciousness, and Jesus said, "Except ye turn, and become as little children, ye shall in no wise enter into the kingdom of heaven" (Matt. 18:3). PH 185

∼199∼

GOD'S LOVE AND OURS

READING: 1 JOHN 4

Since God so loved us, we also ought to love one another. . . . If we love one another, God lives in us and his love is made complete in us.

1 JOHN 4:11–12

God's love for me is inexhaustible, and His love for me is the basis of my love for others. We have to love where we cannot respect and where we must not respect, and this can only be done on the basis of God's love for us. "This is My commandment, That ye love one another, as I have loved you" (John 13:34). OBH 59

Jesus has loved me to the end of all my meanness and selfishness and sin; now, He says, show that same love to others. PH 81

∼200∼

YOU MAY KNOW YOU HAVE ETERNAL LIFE

READING: 1 JOHN 5

I write these things to you who believe in the name of

the Son of God so that you may know that you have eternal life.

1 JOHN 5:13

"The gift *of* God is eternal life" (Rom. 6:23), not the gift *from* God, as if eternal life were a present given by God: It is Himself. CD VOL. 1 139

The life which Jesus Christ exhibited was eternal life, and He says, anyone who believes in Me—commits himself to Me—has that life. To commit myself to Jesus means there is nothing that is not committed. HG 110

"As He is, so are we." The sanctified life is a life that bears a strong family likeness to Jesus Christ, a life that exhibits His virtues, His patience, His love, His holiness. Slowly and surely we learn the great secret of eternal life, which is to know God. OBH 43

∼ 201 ∼

WATCH OUT FOR DECEIVERS

READING: 2 AND 3 JOHN

It has given me great joy to find some of your children walking in the truth, just as the Father commanded us.

2 JOHN 4

Allow nothing to take you away from Jesus Himself, and all other phases of truth will take their right place. GW 106

Beware of turning your back on what you know is true because you do not want it to be real. SHL 60

∽202∽

A Call to Persevere

Reading: Jude

Contend for the faith that was once for all entrusted to the saints.

Jude 3

The Lord can never make a saint out of a good man; He can only make a saint out of three classes of people: the godless man, the weak man, and the sinful man, and no one else; and the marvel of the gospel of God's grace is that Jesus Christ can make us naturally what He wants us to be. HG 76

When a man is born from above, he does not need to pretend to be a saint. He cannot help being one. SSM 30

Oswald Chambers is the author of *My Utmost for His Highest* and many other devotional books. Born in Scotland, he was converted under the preaching of Charles Haddon Spurgeon and became a Baptist evangelist. During World War I he ministered to troops in Egypt, where he died suddenly in 1917 at the age of forty-three.

James R. Adair joined the editorial staff of Scripture Press Publications, Inc., in 1945 after three years as a newspaper reporter in Asheville, North Carolina. Until 1975 he served as editor of *Power for Living* and other Scripture Press Sunday school take-home papers. In 1972 he became founding director of the company's Victor Books Division. He worked for Scripture Press for fifty-one years, during which time he authored or co-authored seven books and compiled eleven others. He and his wife, Virginia, reside in Wheaton, Illinois, and have twin daughters, Mary and Martha.

Harry Verploegh, since his retirement from a Chicago typography firm, has gleaned more than one hundred thousand quotations from noted Christian writers, ten thousand of them from the writings of Oswald Chambers, resulting in seven volumes of the English writer's quotations. Verploegh has also compiled eleven books containing the writings of A. W. Tozer as well as a book of excerpts from the writings of George MacDonald. Harry lives in Carol Stream, Illinois, and he and his late wife, Ruth, are parents of a daughter, Virginia Steinmetz, and a son, Case.